THE PEACE CORPS

Who, How, and Where

THE
PEACE CORPS—
Who, How, and Where

BY

CHARLES E. WINGENBACH

———————◆———————

Preface by

R. SARGENT SHRIVER

Foreword by

SENATOR HUBERT H. HUMPHREY

THE JOHN DAY COMPANY
NEW YORK

New and Revised Edition

To My Mother and Father

ACKNOWLEDGMENTS

In doing this book, I have been helped by many people. Perhaps this is the best way to say thanks.

First, I want to thank my wife, Mary Ann, who patiently corrected and typed the manuscript. I am also grateful to her parents, Bill and Mary Pearce, and to the Clarks, McIntyres, and Pearces of Louisville, Kentucky, who showed me what true Southern hospitality is.

Among my friends, special thanks go to Earl Mazo and Roscoe Drummond, who have helped me with advice and opportunities over the past three years. I thank also Bob Donovan and the other staffers of the New York *Herald Tribune*, Washington Bureau, who have helped in many other ways.

To Steve Hess I am grateful for giving an unknown the chance for a book contract. Publisher Robert W. Hill and Agent Perry Knowlton deserve a prize for patience.

On Capitol Hill, Senator Hubert Humphrey and his hard-working assistant, Win Griffith, have been particularly helpful, as has the charming Senator

Maurine Neuberger. Congressman Henry Reuss also assisted the project.

I would like to express appreciation to Attorney General Robert Kennedy and his information aide, Jack Rosenthal. And further along Pennsylvania Avenue I thank Pierre Salinger, Harris Wofford, and Richard Goodwin of the White House staff.

There is hardly anyone on the Peace Corps staff who did not give aid beyond the call of duty, but at the top of the list are Bill Haddad, Vic Crichton, Gordon Boyce, Pat Kennedy, Sally Bowles, Mitzi Mallina, Tom Matthews, Pete Grothe, Tom Quimby and Jim Moody.

Equal gratitude goes to the private voluntary agencies. In the International Voluntary Services, Dr. J. S. Noffsinger. The American Friends Service Committee—Dr. Clarence Pickett, Steve Carey, Polly Frazier, Ed Wright, and Nancy Duryea. Catholic Relief Services—Bob Melina, Monsignor Joseph Harnett, and Mary O'Hara. And, finally, Reverend James Robinson and Richard McFarland of Crossroads Africa, Dr. Wayland Zwayer of the American Voluntary Agencies Council, and Bill Nighswonger of World Neighbors.

Thanks also to Andy Rice and Frank Land of the Colorado State University Research Foundation.

For putting up with countless requests for information, I'm grateful to Miss Adoreen McCormick and Mrs. Jeanne Burch of the Library of Congress.

CONTENTS

Preface

Accurate information about the Peace Corps is necessary for the continued success of our operations. Mr. Wingenbach's first book about the Corps was helpful to many Americans, and I feel sure that the second edition will reach an even larger audience interested in serving their country and mankind by service in the Peace Corps. I'm grateful to Mr. Wingenbach for his contribution. Without assistance of this type, the Peace Corps could not have grown from a mere idea in March 1961 to a worldwide enterprise in 1963.

R. SARGENT SHRIVER
Director, The Peace Corps

December, 1962

Foreword

The Peace Corps, transformed in a few quick months from dream to reality, is a practical result of President Kennedy's inaugural plea: "Let us begin."

None of us who worked to organize and develop the Peace Corps claim that it will be the final answer to the tensions and miseries of a restless world.

We do believe—deeply and confidently—that the Peace Corps is a vital step toward fulfillment of our goal.

Our goal is becoming more distinct as we witness millions of people in underdeveloped regions of the world rising against the intolerable conditions and miseries of the past. We seek a world in which mankind is relieved of the ancient enemies of freedom and the loyal allies of totalitarianism—poverty, hunger, disease and illiteracy.

The purpose of the Peace Corps is keyed to helping men and women help themselves to security, to progress, to individual dignity. The Peace Corps is not and should never be a mere propaganda gimmick or a weapon of the Cold War. It is and must remain an effective tool for peace and progress throughout the world.

The Peace Corps also offers a new and dramatic dimension to America's concern for the welfare of other peoples and to its efforts to help build the solid foundations for peace.

Peace is not passive; it is not merely the absence of violence. There can be no peace for the middle-aged woman in Burma suffering from malaria. There can be no peace for the emaciated teen-age boy in India who survives—barely—on several hundred calories a day. There can be no peace for the illiterate and unskilled tribesman in Tanganyika bound to a quagmire of want.

The United States today is committed to placing a man on the moon in this decade. For that exciting goal, we have a plan, a program—and a budget.

Is one man on the moon any more important than half of mankind in misery?

To lift mankind to higher levels of decency and dignity, we also need a commitment, a plan and a program.

We must offer to the underdeveloped regions of the world more than cash and high-level technical advisers. We must offer to the peoples of those lands desperately needed operational skills and the training to allow those skills to endure and multiply among local citizens.

Under our new commitment and program, we must also offer the hand of friendship. The day is gone when the United States will deal only with the governments of nations and when well-paid, well-housed American personnel deal with local "natives" as superiors.

Our efforts overseas today need a touch of humility. Our people must approach the people of other lands as equals, as partners, as fellow human beings willing to share the skills and work needed to build a better life for all.

That is the task of Peace Corps volunteers. They will not work and live in American ghettos of luxury in underdeveloped lands. They will share the joys and pains, the frustrations and hopes of the people they seek to serve.

The dream of a Peace Corps is now reality. The need now is for realistic plans to give force to the Peace Corps, and realistic understanding of the challenge to the Peace Corps and its members.

Charles Wingenbach helps provide that understanding in this book.

The American people must seek to understand both the opportunities and problems of the Peace Corps. They must reject both the mocking skepticism and the head-in-the-clouds type of optimism so often expressed for the Peace Corps.

They must be prepared for some mistakes, some failures and even some casualties as the Peace Corps develops and grows.

But more important, they must have the vision to see the magnificent potential of the Peace Corps.

The real power of the United States is not in the

Government. It is not in the modern weapons of destruction or the tools of industry.

The real power of America is in the people, in the compassion of individual Americans for others and in their capacity of skills and dedication to help others.

The sooner we put that power to work in the world's zone of misery, the sooner peace will be secured.

That is the purpose of the Peace Corps. That is the goal of America. That is the hope of man.

HUBERT H. HUMPHREY

INTRODUCTION

HISTORY OF THE PEACE CORPS
MOVEMENT

You will live in a small wooden house, sleep on the floor on a bamboo mat, with a pillow stuffed with rice grain and a mosquito net to protect you from the swarm of bloodthirsty mosquitoes. The heavy humid heat and the hard bed will not be comfortable. You will go down to the well to get water to wash your face. Make sure to boil it befort drinking it to avoid malaria. . . . Soon the sun will turn extremely hot and you will be expected to work in the field in the hot sun with the other men, because only when you are ready to share in the work of the people you want to live with will you be able to be one of them.

Let us pretend that you will teach—your students will come with just a piece of chalk and a slate to no schoolhouse . . . those that don't have a slate can trace letters with their fingers in the dust. . . . In the monsoon you will suffer from the damp weather but nothing changes. . . . The work is the same, only now leeches will cling to you; worms, frogs and snakes will be numerous. The roof will probably leak and all the time you will

17

have to eat with your fingers as other utensils are nonexistent.

Will you be able to take all this?

KHIN KHIN HLA, a Burmese student [1]

Apparently President John F. Kennedy was aware of the hardships when he set up the Peace Corps by executive order in March, 1961. Select American men and women are to journey to distant lands "to help [them] meet their urgent needs for skilled manpower." [2]

Public response, encouraged by Mr. Kennedy's appeals during the 1960 campaign, has been largely favorable. Students on campuses across the nation—and many of their elders—see the idea as a revolutionary concept that will reawaken America to what they consider our lost national purpose: the "task of bringing to man that decent way of life which is the foundation of freedom and a condition of peace." [3]

Skeptics are not hard to find, however, and here the issue has made some strange bedfellows. Former Vice-President Nixon called the Peace Corps "a haven for draft dodgers," and one conservative Washington columnist has ridiculed it as a Children's Crusade. Radio Moscow, meanwhile, insists that it is just a cynical front for U. S. intelligence agents to infiltrate and re-enslave the former West-

[1] New York *Herald Tribune*, March 27, 1961.
[2] From the statement accompanying the executive order, March 1, 1961.
[3] *Ibid.*

ern colonies; the leftist Pan-Africa People's Conference has condemned the proposal on similar grounds.

Not a New Idea

What many of the Peace Corps' supporters and critics do not realize is this: the idea is not new. It is more than a century old at least, and some traces of it could probably be found in the missions Alexander the Great sent to the Orient. What is more, it has been tried—with varying degrees of success *and* failure—by governments and private agencies in recent times.

In 1850, British writers Thomas Carlyle and John Ruskin advocated "industrial regiments . . . to fight the bogs and wildernesses at home and abroad. . . ." [4] Ruskin attempted to implement the idea by having Oxford dons and students build a road nearby, but it was a dismal flop.

The Old World was crumbling, and the United States, under the first Roosevelt, had temporarily emerged from isolation when, in 1904, philosopher William James proposed to the Universal Peace Congress in Boston that draft-age young men be put to work building, not destroying. James called his project "the moral equivalent of war," and said that the newly directed discipline would produce "toughness without callousness, authority with as little criminal cruelty as possible, and painful work done cheerily because the duty is temporary, and

[4] Thomas Carlyle, *Latter-Day Pamphlets* (New York: Harper, 1850), pp. 42–43.

threatens not, as now, to degrade the whole remainder of one's life." [5]

He and his contemporaries had seen the example of the Spanish-American War veterans who stayed behind in the Philippines to teach and work in the barrios. But they realized some of their wildest hopes when, a generation later, President Franklin D. Roosevelt inaugurated his three-pronged youth resources effort: the Civilian Conservation Corps (CCC), the Work Projects Administration (WPA), and the National Youth Administration (NYA). These emergency work-relief and vocational training programs snowballed because, in the depression economy of the early thirties, nearly 14 million workers were unemployed, and approximately 30 per cent of these were youths between the ages of sixteen and twenty-four. A "vicious circle" worked against national recovery—young men could not obtain jobs to learn skills, yet employers refused to hire anyone without skill and experience. Work camps were set up, and the unskilled did everything from planting tree seedlings to constructing bridges and dams.

How useful this was in practical terms will probably be debated for years to come. But many CCC veterans, ranging in occupation from a Minnesota congressman to a Vermont truck driver, say that it gave real purpose and work to jobless men who might otherwise have degenerated into the same

[5] William James, *Memories and Studies* (New York: Longmans, 1912), pp. 290–291.

sort of restless mobs that catapulted Hitler to power during those same years.

Programs of this nature were necessarily temporary and limited in scope. Churches and private voluntary agencies had been working in the field long before the Great Depression forced the United States and several European countries to enlist the services of their youthful citizens. National recovery, though, formed only a small part of their agenda. In addition, financed by private contributions and government grants, their projects have sent thousands of men and women abroad to instruct illiterate peasants in sanitation and the three R's, better ways to farm and to conserve natural resources, and now perform a hundred other community services as well.

How the Project Began

The embryo existed in the work of the private agencies, but Project Peace Corps is the child both of chance and of hard work by its never-say-die supporters. Exactly how or when it was born, no one knows.

In 1954, Heinz Rollman, a North Carolina industrialist and wartime refugee from Hitler's Germany, wrote a book titled *World Construction*, which he mailed to government officials and opinion makers throughout the free world. His principal proposals were a 3-million-man "Peace Army" of draftees to work in underdeveloped nations and an increase of foreign exchange students to five million. During the 1960 political campaign, President Eisenhower derided Democrat Kennedy's Peace Corps as a warmed-over version of ideas originated by Heinz Rollman, at the time a Republican candidate for Congress.

Little else was heard of the idea for the next couple of years after the distribution of Mr. Rollman's book. In 1957, a group of Congressmen visited the Southeast Asian nation of Cambodia to see how U. S. taxpayers' money was being used in the foreign aid program.

One day they drove for miles along a new modern highway without spotting a single motorist. A solitary farmer trudged down the edge of the deserted road, his water buffalo in tow. Yet $30 million in American aid, plus valuable time and technical know-how, had been poured into the project.

Further on, however, they came to a village in the jungle. An elementary school stood in the clearing, and four young Americans told the visiting dignitaries how they had built it with primitive tools and manual labor. Just a short time before, the four had been schoolteachers back in the States; now they were going from village to village, teaching an Asian people how to read and write.

Their example set one member of the party, Representative Henry S. Reuss of Wisconsin, to thinking how the $30 million spent on the highway might better have been used to finance the work of thousands like them. Later, at Cornell University, he expanded the idea into a proposal for a

Point 4 youth corps. The students were so enthusiastic that thereafter he buttonholed everyone who would listen to him about it.

However, he was not the only prominent figure thinking along these lines. The Peace Corps' present Director, R. Sargent Shriver, then a Chicago educator and one-time leader of the Experiment in International Living, returned that same year from a swing through Asia to present a similar idea to President Eisenhower as an extension of the Administration's People-to-People program, but nothing came of it.

Meanwhile, Dr. Tom Dooley's work in Laos had begun to generate a lot of public interest. By late 1959, the situation had jelled sufficiently for Congressman Reuss to introduce legislation in the House for a study of the proposal; the late Senator Richard L. Neuberger of Oregon introduced a companion measure in the Senate.

The wind was almost knocked out of the project even before it began. When the Reuss bill came up before the House Appropriations Committee, Chairman Otto Passman of Louisiana, a perennial foreign aid foe, struck out the $10,000 budget for the study. Peace Corps supporters were dismayed, but Reuss went to work at once on Passman, who finally gave in and agreed that if the Senate restored the money, he would go along with the joint conference. Senator Hubert H. Humphrey of Minnesota sent an urgent plea to the Senate Appropriations Committee chairman, Carl Hayden of Arizona, and the funds were put back in the bill.

Congress authorized the study in June, 1960, and that November the International Co-operation Administration (ICA) farmed out the contract to Colorado State University.

Senator Humphrey was an early backer of the Corps. Impressed by the success of the Quakers (American Friends Service Committee), he had tested its appeal before college groups on several occasions in 1957. The time came, however, when he tired of reading studies and longed instead for action. In the spring of 1960, the Senator detailed a foreign relations adviser, Peter Grothe, to see whether the project was actually feasible enough to start work on it right away. Grothe spent six weeks interviewing private agency workers and digging through available material, and he also got an unexpected assist from two Yale and Harvard graduate students who had been unaware of the Reuss efforts.

In his final report, young Grothe conservatively estimated that 10,000 volunteers could be sent into the field within four or five years; the Senator, often accused of radical leanings, slashed this down still further to 5,000 on a trial basis. Then on June 16, he formally proposed to the Senate that a U. S. Peace Corps be set up immediately. A deluge of favorable mail poured in, dwarfing both the U-2 incident and Fidel Castro in interest.

How and when did John F. Kennedy decide to adopt the proposal? Many of his aides insist that it was a fluke, but the evidence indicates that it was deliberately timed for maximum political appeal.

Several in the Americans for Democratic Action (A.D.A.) wing of the party have said that after battling Senator Humphrey's grip on Democratic liberals, Kennedy thought that the idealism of the Peace Corps could help swing still-reluctant Stevensonians and perhaps a Rockefeller Republican or two into his camp. The New Frontier hopeful probably also remembered how the New Deal's Franklin D. Roosevelt capitalized on the CCC in his own first Presidential race.

In February, 1960, Kennedy was first queried on the Corps while appearing on the New York television program, *College News Conference*. He admitted that he didn't know much about it, but when he returned to Washington, he instructed his staff to work on the idea.

The next link in the chain of events was seven months later. In September, after Kennedy had won the nomination, Peter Grothe took the Humphrey proposal to Archibald Cox, at the time the candidate's chief speech writer and now the U. S. Solicitor-General. Advisers in the Kennedy brain trust had already pointed out the idea's potential, both as a new foreign policy breakthrough and as an election issue, and the Humphrey "Youth Peace Corps" was incorporated into certain future papers on the subject by Kennedy's advisers.

Chester Bowles, a one-time liberal dark-horse candidate and now Under Secretary of State, discussed the Peace Corps with Kennedy and made several campaign speeches about it. Sam and

Nancy Bowles, his son and daughter-in-law, are in Nigeria as teachers.

Once made, the proposal caught like wildfire—and under the most unlikely circumstances. It was a tired and dispirited Kennedy campaign crew that, having arrived on the campus long after midnight on October 14, 1960, listened as their chief asked 10,000 University of Michigan students to give as much as ten years of their lives to serving mankind. The audience responded with an ovation, and despite the early hour some hardy souls began forming on the spot committees to push the project.

Barnstorming from city to city, Kennedy let the issue simmer a while and went on to other topics. However, both he and his opponent met more than an occasional question on the Peace Corps, although newspaper coverage of the Michigan speech was meager. And, in late October, Army General James M. Gavin, now U. S. Ambassador to France, spoke of the idea to the Nuclear Energy Regional Advisory Council in Miami, and then took it up with the Democratic candidate.

Kennedy's timing reportedly caught the Nixon camp off base. The Vice-President's unenthusiastic treatment of such ideas disgruntled many Rockefeller Republicans who still considered the liberal Governor of New York their party's best bet. An adviser on African affairs testifies that in the early stages of the campaign he gave Nixon a study outlining a youth corps, but, as it turned out later, the plan was shelved. In the meantime Robert Bowie, policy planning chief under the late Secretary of State Dulles, urged a Senate subcommittee to enlist 1,000 college graduates a year in a Foreign Service junior technical assistance corps; later President Eisenhower's Committee on Information Activities Abroad suggested a similar long-term overseas youth aid program. A close aide to the former President said that the proposal was brought up at White House conferences and vetoed, mainly on objections from the Pentagon; he added, however, that both Eisenhower and Nixon spiritually liked the concept, but the grave reservations they had for its success overruled their sympathies.

Ironically, rumors of an impending Nixon proposal of a youth aid program are said to have spurred Kennedy's headline-making speech November 2nd in San Francisco. But to this day Nixon vehemently denies that he ever had any intentions of the kind. Nor will the new President's staff officially admit any more than mere coincidence in his choice of Nixon's home state for the project's formal launching.

The San Francisco speech was written by Theodore (Ted) Sorenson—then and now Kennedy's right-hand man—and Richard Goodwin, a White House expert on Latin America. Kennedy broadened the Humphrey-Reuss concept to include women and older persons, and he also offered a draft exemption to volunteers. This last caused him no end of trouble and earned Nixon's scorn for the proposal.

The choice of the name "Peace Corps" indicates an uncertainty in Kennedy's mind as to the scope of the project. He gave it that title in San Francisco, but as late as January, 1961, the President-elect's headquarters in New York called it the "International Youth Service Agency," the name suggested by Professor Max F. Millikan of Massachusetts Institute of Technology. The present title was partly a concession to Senator Humphrey, who argued that we need to restore to the word peace the true meaning Communist jargon has stolen from it. And it shows Kennedy's return to his original stand that the Peace Corps should have no arbitrary age limits.

For a time after the election, little was heard of the Peace Corps. Compared with the delicate tasks of choosing cabinet officers and smoothing the transition from the old regime to the new, the project was relatively low on the priority list of things that had to be done.

Nevertheless, a minor miracle of organization took place. Sargent Shriver and Harris Wofford, later made White House liaison with the Peace Corps, were given the job of making and co-ordinating plans for the new agency. Before half of the first Hundred Days was up, the President had created it by executive fiat. For such a controversial program, this was bold by anyone's standards. The awesome F.D.R. had waited for Congress to authorize the CCC; Kennedy first gave the order and later asked the jealous solons to approve it. It was reasoned that, to avoid red tape and to give it the greatest impact, this was the only course if the program was ever to get underway. But the new Chief Executive recognized the political hazards involved and tried to get former Republican President Herbert Hoover to act as the program's chairman. When Hoover gingerly declined for equally political reasons, Vice-President Lyndon B. Johnson, a past master in handling Capitol Hill, was named to head an advisory council drawn from many professional walks of life.

The Future

Now that the Peace Corps is off the ground, many questions about it come to mind. What are its prospects? What will be its role at home and abroad? What dangers and requirements lie in the way of success?

Most important, what sort of people are being recruited? What will be their training? Experienced missionaries and businessmen fear that the popular new government agency, eager to confound its critics, will send relatively untrained, comfort-conscious youths to touchy new nations as shirt-sleeve ambassadors. Are these fears justified? Can these "kids" accomplish something that has baffled veteran diplomats—namely, how to get through to the hearts and minds of the world's underprivileged majority?

To these questions, there is no better answer than the initial year's experience of the Peace Corps itself, and the vast experience of the private voluntary agencies. They have come up against the same obstacles, and what they have learned has set many of the guidelines for the Peace Corps.

This book is *not* an attempt to recruit volunteers or to garner support for the Peace Corps. What *is* attempted is a serious and frank appraisal of the work that has been done and the work to be done. Its simultaneous purpose is to present the problems and the promise of the new federal agency. If, in doing so, this book persuades the reader to join or to support the Peace Corps, then well and good.

CHARLES E. WINGENBACH

PART ONE

———◆———

TRIAL AND ERROR

CHAPTER 1

THE NEED AND
THE EXPERIENCE

The young doctor studies a sickly child. He turns to the mother, and says, "The boy has malaria. But a few injections, good sleep and patient care, and he'll be out with his playmates in no time. Be sure to bring him back tomorrow, señora." The Indian girl nods in understanding, but watching her leave, the doctor knows he has won only half the battle.

She takes the child into the waiting room, where the ancient grandmother greets her grimly. But they are silent as they walk home.

As they stoop to enter the airless adobe hut, the old woman's voice breaks out in scorn. "The white man has fed you a lot of tales. But you believed him and his mission padres. Would you take the cloves and goat's milk to the hag of the hill? No, you think it is superstitious and unscientific! Ha, what does science know of the evil powers of the witch? In revenge she has put Juanito on his death-bed. The foreigner can do nothing for him, no matter what he says. Will you still defy all the traditions of our ancestors? Must your child and our whole village be cursed so that we will have no rest after we die? Come, we will go and promise the hag we will not take Juanito to the hospital."

Finally, the terror-stricken young widow gives in, and the two leave to pay tribute to the unknown.

Two days later, Juanito dies. It is God's will.

Thousands like Juanito die every day, and superstition is but one of the reasons why. And, like the young doctor, many would-be Samaritans have lent elbow grease and know-how only to find their efforts stymied at every turn. Not a few have wondered if the effort is really worth while.

Perhaps it is the "fellowship of pain" that Tom Dooley often spoke of in trying to explain why he sacrificed a brilliant career in order to heal the penniless sick of Asian jungles. Or perhaps it is to spread the benefits of modern industry and agriculture to an awakening African continent which still uses the technology of medieval Europe. Whatever the reason, private American citizens have considered this work so important that, since 1939, they have contributed over $3 billion to voluntary agencies providing such aid to about 100 nations.

As if this were not enough, the Kennedy Administration has since established the Peace Corps. Its objective is "work assistance" at the grass-roots level. For the most part, Corpsmen will be volunteers fresh out of college, not seasoned diplomats or technical experts. The Point 4 concept was a new and revolutionary chapter in American foreign policy. Even more so is a government-sponsored Peace Corps.

However, there is nothing new in the use of semiskilled youth for overseas assistance. The Quakers (American Friends Service Committee) started their program even before the coals of World War I had had a chance to cool. And in 1960 the UNESCO Coordination Committee listed 133 work camps in 32 countries, with 80 different organizations as patrons.

Experience in the field is vast, but so is the need. The idea that top-level programming is the cure-all for the world's ills is as outdated as Henry Ford's Model T. In 1953 Dr. Mottram P. Torre, consultant to the Mutual Security Agency, gave this testimony: "The few failures due to the lack of technical competence were related to a person with the wrong kind of skills being recruited to do the job rather than a person who lacked technical competence. *Many of the men were overqualified and had skills far beyond the need of the immediate situation. . . .*" [1] The moral is that villages still at the fifteenth century level have little use for the highly mechanized skills of the Atomic Age. The voluntary agencies have pioneered in filling the more practical needs.

The purposes of a Peace Corps type of operation are many and varied. The basic one, though, is "institution building." The Western tradition of vol-

---

[1] *The Administration of Technical Assistance: Growth in the Americas,* by Philip M. Glick (Chicago: University of Chicago Press, 1957), p. 146.

untary service is foreign to many cultures, and a developing nation lacking it is hard put to erect the necessary framework for a healthy political, economic and social life. Example by actual physical co-operation in self-help can, therefore, be very valuable since it does not smack of the patronizing condescension that so often accompanies foreign aid. Concretely, this means that an educated young citizen of a foreign nation working alongside his peer from America will acquire enough respect for honest sweat and toil to build up functioning private and government organisms, instead of mass bureaucracies.

A successful private agency doing just this is the International Voluntary Services. Since 1953, IVS has sent over 200 youths as junior technicians to Africa, Indochina and the Near East. Most of its volunteers grew up on family farms and bring practical skills to their work. These young men are used to tinkering around with engines, repairing tools, using simple carpentry to fix up an old barn and other rudimentary techniques that aren't ordinarily acquired through formal schooling. However, all IVS team members must be college graduates, and they must tackle a variety of tasks ranging from animal husbandry to rigging a makeshift well.

There is no room, on the other hand, for mass projects like leaf raking, ditch digging or others which seem to fascinate those who see the Peace Corps as a glorified overseas CCC. The new nations have more than enough unemployed laborers who can be used for these purposes, and the surest way to scuttle the new foreign aid concept would be to send droves of eager, adventure-seeking youths to add to this pool. Originally, even in the Peace Corps, some viewed it first and foremost as cultural exchange, and only incidentally as a hard-headed humanitarian effort to help the Nigerian or the Indonesian to raise his standard of living and gain effectiveness in new techniques. If the private agencies have learned anything, it is that people who are trying to pull themselves up by their boot-straps have only contempt for that sort of naïveté. Moreover, they would have good reason to suspect the motives behind any large-scale invasion by for-eigners who mouth idealism but offer no practical solutions to their problems.

This last point is important. IVS and other groups have found it best not to assign more than five or ten Americans to any one project, and these must be matched by local "counterparts" or work associ-ates. For example, an American public health vol-unteer in Laos would work side by side with a *medecin indochinois,* who may have the equivalent of grade school education plus a smattering of medical know-how. The Laotian learns by doing, and the American gets an understanding of the average villager's special needs and quirks, and vice versa. No amount of mere cultural exchange could accomplish that.

The Communist Challenge

Another category of well-wisher is the "cru-sader." Whether right or left, he wants to use the

Peace Corps as a new U. S. propaganda arm. The conservative argues something like this: "Since the taxpayer is footing the bill, our boys and girls should sell our American free-enterprise system abroad." For the left, it's "a bold new program to counter Russian advances in the underdeveloped countries of the world."

But, as Al Smith once said, no matter how you slice it, it's still baloney. Either approach would mean the kiss of death for the Peace Corps in neutralist Africa and Asia or even allied Latin America. No foreign politician sensitive to the public pulse would dare welcome Americans under such a guise.

On the other hand, the Cold War *does* exist. It is obvious that success in aid projects will inevitably benefit the foreign policy of the bloc sponsoring them. An African aid adviser to Khrushchev, Professor I. I. Potekhin, frankly admitted Russia's propaganda aims. "One of our major tasks," he said, "[is] to establish the truth about Africa—not because we want it, but because we want to help the Africans understand their history better." American reporter Marvin Kalb asked him if this meant in terms of Marxism-Leninism. "There is no other truth," Potekhin replied. "And I can assure you that no one working in this institute has any other truth." [2]

No better showcase for Soviet bloc assistance exists than the former French-African colony of

[2] "Russia's Own 'Peace Corps' for Africa," *The Reporter*, April 13, 1961.

Guinea. Yet, when the Guinean government asked the Eisenhower Administration for technical assistance and loans, they got a cold shoulder. The reasons were obvious: when France saw that Guinea would not toe the line, she withdrew all her civil servants at once and the African nation teetered on total collapse. The United States, anxious not to displease her proud ally, went along in everything, and Guinea, spurned, turned to the East.

Reverend William Coffin, Yale University chaplain and Peace Corps adviser, headed a work-camp project in Guinea for Operation Crossroads-Africa. This is the account he gave of his experience:

"We Crossroaders were practically the first Americans in Guinea. Sékou Touré welcomed us, as he and his people are anxious to reverse what they regard as a hostile American press.

"Communist technicians are everywhere. The Russians said they had twelve teachers in secondary schools, but I only met three of them. Since I speak Russian, I got to know them fairly well. None were over twenty-three, but strangely they were ill at ease with Guineans, which is remarkable considering the favor they enjoy there.

"The Red propaganda effort is at the point of saturation. Radio Peking beams loud and clear, and only regional stations can be heard better. You can hear Voice of America, but not too well. The bookstores in Conakry are filled with slick, readable Soviet bloc magazines, and I saw an East German 'White Paper' on Western imperialism.

"People ask why Guinea is important, why Guineans are hostile to our country. The answer is Guineans do not think in Cold War terms of East and West. For them, it's North and South. North is white European colonialism, and South is black Africa. Perhaps because they have had no adverse involvement with Communism, Guineans cannot understand what the Cold War means.

"We Americans have too often asked too much of Guinea, and given too little. The U.S.A. has been regarded as overloyal to her European colonial allies. Neither have our earlier feelers toward Guinea been any more judicious. When we finally got around to recognizing that Guinea exists, the International Cooperation Administration (ICA) demanded full diplomatic immunity for all our technicians. The Russians and Chinese had asked no favors, so Touré angrily refused.

"Jim Crow is the worst albatross around our neck, and it's kind of embarrassing when we have to wear it and try to talk to Africa at the same time. Twice I realized just what this means—once as a white American in Guinea, and later when I was jailed with other Freedom Riders in Montgomery.

"Any Peace Corpsman who goes to Guinea will have to know what he's talking about. He should know Marxist dialectics and have a thorough background in the issues behind the news. This means segregation in our country as well as the history of Russian vetoes in the UN. He must not attempt to proselytize, but there will be questions and he should be prepared to answer them."

Both President Kennedy and Director Shriver

have stressed over and over again the humanitarian emphasis of the Peace Corps, and the private agencies know from long experience that no other objective can succeed. But, as Reverend Coffin suggested, American representatives cannot forever turn the other cheek when quizzed by curious neutralists or professional agitators. Otherwise, they will lose face; in face-conscious countries, that would be just as fatal as blatant propaganda.

American Friends Service Committee official Stephen Carey agrees that it is a delicate task, but he thinks that the quiet example of unselfish work will, in the long run, be more valuable than any amount of persuasion. Numerous cases can be cited to back up his claim. At the time the Suez crisis exploded in 1956, an IVS team of two was working an experimental farm in Egypt. The villagers stood in long queues to see them off, and Moslem fathers who had worked with them in the fields paid the young Americans unusual tribute by naming their children after them. After the Suez conflict was over, President Gamal Abdel Nasser asked IVS to send the two back, along with ten more like them. The first Crossroads group had a similar experience. When they arrived at an airport in West Africa the air was heavy with suspicion. One young African would help with the luggage of his Negro guests only; when he found he had been carrying a white girl's suitcase, he tossed it across the ground. Luckily, American tempers were held in check and an even more unpleasant incident was avoided. In three weeks, however, whites and blacks were working together, and the African apologized to the girl.

Terrors on the Domestic Front

Foreign-aid workers readily admit that while they will gladly take on any number or size of difficulties abroad, they quail at the thought of the twin terrors back home: government red tape and the Congressional appropriations system. Many good ideas start in the flush of idealism and courage, only to be ground between the two and emerge as faceless, expensive and repetitive bureaucracies. For that reason, the private agencies are reluctant to surrender their independence; one spokesman expressed the fear that the Peace Corps will swallow up its parents and become a "junior ICA."

Most red tape stems from the awkward system of Congressional appropriations for government projects. The routine seems deceptively necessary and logical, even simple on the face of it. But a new agency inherits the procedures, good and bad, of its predecessor, as well as a welter of confusing advice from the whole federal structure. In Washington, the agency receives reports and estimates from the field, plus private estimates of needed projects by the host government. In turn it has to anticipate difficulties by trying to determine in advance just how much it can allocate to each sector. Then the statistics must pass through the sensitive fingers of the Budget Bureau and under the politically minded eyes of the members of Congress. More often than not, Congress sharply reduces funds, and may even begin the whole rigmarole of questioning whether the agency is necessary after all. Or a Congressman may add a pet project or two, while cutting the money for another project which an involved consultation between field chiefs, the host government, interagency conferees and dozens of others had already judged imperative. As one wag remarked, it is usually for "reasons known only to God and the constituents back in Podunk."

Harlan Cleveland, the present Assistant Secretary of State for International Organization Affairs, summed up the problem neatly: "We know in our hearts that we are in the world for keeps, yet we are still tackling twenty-year problems with five-year plans staffed with two-year personnel working with one-year appropriations." A former ICA project chief differed with this judgment in only one respect, namely that today's problems will take far longer than twenty years to solve.

The situation may improve, however, with both a sympathetic President and sympathetic Congressional leaders in the saddle. But even this is no guarantee. When he first recommended the Marshall Plan, President Harry Truman asked for long-term appropriations. Congress judged that his request would unduly curtail the powers of review which it so jealously guards, and the present one-year system was retained.

Specific Needs

Why, despite certain misgivings about domestic

43

and foreign obstacles, do most voluntary agencies insist that the Peace Corps is necessary? Just how necessary is it?

Half the world is in poverty, hunger and disease. Over two thirds of the people of Africa, Asia, and Latin America are illiterate. As Senator Humphrey told Congress last year, no nation can compete in this highly competitive world without a literate population. In fact, though, many social scientists agree that a concerted effort could wipe out a substantial number of so-called population problems. The rich nations continue to get richer, but the poorer nations become still poorer daily. Someone once remarked that it is only when one has encountered the smell of death, the paralysis of despair, and the passions of frustrations working among a whole people that the total physical reality of the problem comes home to him.

The peoples of these nations are not standing still and will not. Colonialism is fading away, but the problems arising in its place make it seem pale by comparison. Lack of an adequate elite is pushing the emerging nations to their limit; if not remedied, extremist solutions will find favor and nations that could have formed a buffer third force will end up as mere pawns of the two giant blocs. It may seem a cliché to say that world peace itself is at stake, but the evidence provided by the Congo and Cuba shows it to be nothing more than the truth.

The human tragedy is worst of all. In one area of Taiwan alone, 80 per cent of the population—men, women and children—were found to be afflicted with crippling goiters. Simple medical techniques and early care could prevent or reduce the disease. In another region, the Catholic Relief Services came across thousands of peasant families who lacked even the simplest of bedding for the damp monsoon season. All that was required was a cotton-processing machine to make "footans," a five-pound cotton quilt. These do-it-yourself methods preserved the health of the people and released part of their meager resources for other family necessities.

The urgency of the need has been underscored by the Peace Corps' reception in underdeveloped countries. Speaking of his world tour in 1961, Director Shriver told an audience at De Paul University:

> Prime Minister Nehru asked us for agricultural extension workers to help meet India's staggering food deficiency. Gandhi himself had said India teems with millions who have to go *without* two meals a day and to whom the only form in which God dare appear is food. . . .
>
> Prime Minister Nkrumah of Ghana asked for plumbers, teachers, and electricians. "Send us teachers," he said, "teachers of science and math and of all subjects—teachers for our elementary schools and our secondary schools and our universities. And send them," he asked, "by August!"
>
> U Nu in Burma wants health workers—sanitation engineers, nurses and nurses' aids, doctors, dental technicians, just to mention a few—and he

45

needs them desperately to help his people lift the burden of disease from their lives.

The leaders of Nigeria—Prime Minister Azikiwe, Sir Tafewa Balewa, and Sardona of Sukutu—unanimously requested teachers. A similar request came from President García of the Philippines . . . [who] has asked the Peace Corps—and we have agreed—to send 300 *teachers' aids* to stem the current deterioration of English instruction. . . .

The problems are immense when viewed in their entirety. But efforts on an individual, grass-roots level have been undertaken, and some of the more pressing hardships have been relieved. While greater resources is not the only solution, it certainly must be regarded as a principal one. The private voluntary agencies simply have not got and cannot by themselves supply what is needed, and this is where the Peace Corps steps into the picture. The vast ability of the Federal Government to enlist adequate funds and trained personnel seems the only answer. What the private agencies *are* certain of is that the U. S. Peace Corps must be maintained on a permanent, expanding basis.

CHAPTER 2

THE FIRST YEAR:
CONTROVERSY, TRAGEDY,
AND ACCOLADES

Since its founding in March, 1961, the Peace Corps
has had its share of growing pains. As Director
Sargent Shriver noted, the major ones were incidents which "gave ammunition to critics who saw
in the Peace Corps a haven for bearded beatniks,
confused liberals, and impractical idealists . . .
[and] who contended that sending young people
overseas to dabble in foreign policy would create
a continuing series of embarrassing incidents." [1]

The first was the case of a bearded twenty-one-
year-old sociology graduate of Brandeis University.
During the 1960 Christmas holidays, he had at-
tended a Rotary Club showing in Miami, Florida,
of the controversial film, *Operation Abolition*. The
film portrays the unfavorable reception given the
House Un-American Activities Committee during
its hearings in San Francisco. Himself a registered

[1] *Saturday Review*, May 19, 1962.

Republican, the young man regarded "Operation Abolition" as a smear of liberal student and labor groups, and he demonstrated his disdain by interrupting the Rotary meeting. He was ejected bodily from the hall.

He later apologized for his actions and shaved the beard as well, but the Rotarians were not so easily mollified. A howl of protest went up when his picture appeared in local newspapers as a Peace Corps trainee at Pennsylvania State University. At the same time, the Miami Draft Board refused to defer him as a potential Peace Corps teacher in the Philippines.

Although the Peace Corps was bombarded with demands for the trainee's dismissal, Sargent Shriver insisted that his fitness for overseas assignment would be decided only after he had been fully tested, not on the basis of a single incident.

The upshot of the case was that late in September, along with 24 other hopefuls, this trainee flunked out of the University's training program.

A Postcard and a Proud New Nation

Hard on the heels of this incident came a still more embarrassing *faux pas*. A young volunteer from Massachusetts had barely arrived in Nigeria when she decided to communicate her impressions of the new African nation to a friend back home. Her mistakes were two: she used a postcard, and then lost it on the campus of Ibadan University at a bad time. Otherwise, her candid note was little different from many of the observations made by newcomers to Africa's shores. It read:

Dear . . . . ,

Don't be furious at getting a card. I promise a letter next time. I wanted you to see the incredible and fascinating city we were in. With all the training we had had, we were really not prepared for the squalor and absolutely primitive living conditions rampant both in the cities and the bush.

We had no idea about what "underdeveloped" meant. It really is a revelation and once we got over the initial, horrified shock, a very rewarding experience. Everyone except us lives in the streets, cooks in the streets, sells in the streets and even goes to the bathroom in the streets. The university is great fun, and it is something to be a foreign student anyway and especially to be the only white students in an all-African university. I just hope that they don't repeat last year's Lumumba riots.

Please write. We are excessively cut off here from the rest of the world.

The addressee wasn't "furious at getting a card," but 200 African students—not the 1,500 reported by the newspapers—were when they read the American trainee's criticism. News of the offensive postcard circulated throughout the university and Nigeria; the Students' Union denounced the recently arrived Peace Corpsmen as "agents of imperialism" and called for their expulsion. The

49

exaggerated early press reports immediately made the incident front page news all over the world.

Once again criticism poured into Peace Corps headquarters in Washington, and the least of the demands was for the girl's resignation. However, she anticipated the growing storm and coupled an apology to her Nigerian hosts with an offer to resign. Shriver refused to make her a sacrificial lamb for her indiscretion, and her offer was declined.

Although the episode could easily have crippled the new agency, Nigeria's political leaders and Peace Corps officials bent over backwards to calm tempers on both sides. The country's new Governor-General, Nnamdi Azikiwe, exchanged views with the girl and reiterated his support of the Peace Corps. But as her usefulness in Nigeria was severely curtailed by the notoriety, she was transferred back to Washington and later assigned to work in Puerto Rico. Her marriage a few months later terminated her Peace Corps service.

Since the incident, the Peace Corps has returned to public favor in Nigeria by dint of hard work, and still more volunteers have gone to work in the country.

A Misunderstanding . . .

Among the thorniest problems before the Peace Corps is the eagerness of its applicants, young and old. It has been emphasized repeatedly that no one is a bona fide volunteer until completion of all stages of selection, testing and training; nevertheless, the zeal of some has outrun their ability to perform.

An elderly widow from Texas was the central figure of a case the Peace Corps calls "unfortunate" in every respect. This sixty-five-year-old former home demonstrator agent touched off a row between Capitol Hill and Peace Corps headquarters when she complained of ill-treatment at the hands of training officials.

In a seven-page, handwritten letter to Republican Senator John Tower, she told of her rejection as a volunteer. She alleged that the real reasons were Peace Corps animosity toward her and her inability to run a mile before breakfast or to swim with her hands tied. She also complained that the other, younger trainees persecuted and cursed her, and she said that living conditions in the camp included rats and lizards as frequent sleeping companions.

The sore point of the case apparently resulted from this trainee's overeagerness to join the Peace Corps. Before going to Puerto Rico, she had prematurely anticipated acceptance by disposing of everything she owned, including home and property, and then shipped the few remaining effects to Brazil. All she had at hand was a suitcase of clothing when the Peace Corps turned her down.

Although Senator Tower criticized this as inhumane treatment of his constituent, the Peace Corps could only reply that all candidates are warned in advance *not* to sell their homes or give up their jobs until *final* acceptance as volunteers.

The shipment of goods, in any case, is the responsibility of the Peace Corps, not the individual.

As to the lady's other complaints, they denied that she had been persecuted, either by the instructors or the trainees, and stated that physical training had always been lightened deliberately for elderly candidates. Rats and lizards, it was admitted, were a part of camp life, but they are a natural hazard of Peace Corps work in the field. In his reply to the Senator, Mr. Shriver insisted that the Selection Board had given this candidate as much consideration as any other trainee received, but that she had not met the needs of the Peace Corps.

. . . a Tragedy

Less than two months after its first anniversary, the Peace Corps experienced its first fatalities. Volunteers Lawrence Radley, of Illinois, and David Crozier, of Missouri, both twenty-two years old, were killed in the crash of a DC-3 airliner in Colombia. They were returning from their Easter vacation to work in a community-development project, when their plane crashed into a mountain near the Colombian west coast. The President of Colombia, Alberto Lleras Camargo, offered personal condolences to American President John F. Kennedy on behalf of his people. Soon afterwards, the Peace Corps decided to commemorate the two with a memorial which would directly benefit the people with whom they had lived and worked the seven months prior to their tragic death; in July,

1962, Director Sargent Shriver dedicated two training sites in Puerto Rico as Camp Crozier and Camp Radley.

. . . and Accolades

In 1961, the vote of the House of Representatives to approve Peace Corps legislation was 288–97; after the initial year of operation, the vote changed to 317–70. This was in spite of the fact that to a Congressional eye, appropriations had mushroomed. In 1961, appropriations were sliced from $40 million to $30 million; 1962 saw Congress vote the full $63.75 million requested to provide for 6,700 volunteers expected to be in the field by June 30, 1963. This was later cut to $59 million by Congress.

The new feeling was that the Peace Corps had withstood its baptism of fire well. One of the early foes of the new agency, conservative Republican Senator Barry Goldwater, expressed official Washington's feeling this way: "I think that the Peace Corps is beginning to remove the doubts from the doubters' minds. I have been impressed with the quality of the young men and women that have been going into it. At first I thought that it would advance work for a group of beatniks, but this is not so. As a businessman, I know that two years overseas experience will be invaluable and rewarding. I'll back it all the way."

The reaction overseas has been a hearty but cautious welcome, tempered by the skepticism of age-old experience. Vice-President Emanuel Pelaez of the Philippines made no bones about the prevailing attitude in countries that, though new in nationhood, are ancient in misery. He welcomed a group of Peace Corps teachers to his country with a frank speech:

The problems which the Peace Corps will find here in the Philippines are not too different from those it will encounter in many countries of Asia and Africa.

They are the problems of underdevelopment, problems that long antedate Communism, neutralism, the Cold War—they are the problems of poverty, ignorance and disease.

I believe I am not shattering any illusions when I say that those problems will not disappear with the coming of the Peace Corps. But certainly you can help; certainly you can make a significant contribution towards overcoming them.

We have a saying in Tagalog.[2] "Ang bato man na matigas ay maaagnas din so kapapatak ng ulan— Even the hardest stone will wear away under constant drops of rain."

Your labors in our fields and barrios, in our schoolhouses and community centers, will be like those constant drops of rain, slowly but surely eroding the boulders of poverty, ignorance and disease which block the road to greatness and prosperity for this country.

[2] A Malay-Polynesian dialect, the native language of the Philippines.

APPENDIX

The Box Score—as of June 30, 1962.

Volunteers

AREAS & COUNTRIES	AT WORK	IN TRAINING	MEN	WOMEN	TOTAL
Africa:					
Ghana	51	85	85	51	136
Ivory Coast	—	41	19	22	41
Liberia	—	94	56	38	94
Niger	—	7	6	1	7
Nigeria	109	74	109	74	183
Senegal		6	4	2	6
Sierra Leone	37	59	63	33	96
Somali Republic	—	47	34	13	47
Tanganyika	35	27	35	27	62
Togo	—	31	20	11	31
Tunisia	—	76	69	7	76

55

AREAS & COUNTRIES	AT WORK	IN TRAINING	MEN	WOMEN	TOTAL
Asia:					
Afghanistan	—	13	5	8	13
N. Borneo & Sarawak	—	76	58	18	76
Ceylon	—	48	33	15	48
Cyprus	—	28	28	—	28
India	26	53	66	13	79
Iran	—	48	42	6	48
Malaya	67	—	27	40	67
Nepal	—	73	56	17	73
Pakistan	57	—	39	18	57
Philippines	272	295	261	306	567
Thailand	45	64	71	38	109
Turkey	—	49	35	14	49
The Americas:					
Bolivia	35	54	56	33	89
Brazil	43	—	29	14	43
Chile	63	—	34	29	63
Colombia	103	—	103	—	103

Dominican Republic	—	21	21	—	21
Ecuador	—	123	73	50	123
El Salvador	25	—	21	4	25
Honduras	—	27	23	4	27
British Honduras	—	36	16	20	36
Jamaica	38	—	26	12	38
Peru	—	178	92	86	178
St. Lucia	15	—	8	7	15
Venezuela	23	39	52	10	62
TOTAL 36	1044	1772	1775	1041	2816

Rate of failures among volunteers—June, 1961, to June, 1962

	TRAINEES IN U.S.A.	VOLUNTEERS AT WORK	TOTAL
Total reporting for training	3,125	—	3,125
Total assigned overseas	1,056	1,056	1,056
Total drop-outs: all causes	301	12	313
Restored after separation	4		4
Total on duty June 30, 1962	1,772	1,044	2,816
Net failure	297	12	309
Total rate of failure	9.5%	1.1%	10.6%

58

PART TWO

THE GREAT BOTTLENECK:

SELECTION

AND TRAINING

CHAPTER 1

WHO SHOULD SERVE?

WANTED

Overseas Workers—Men and Women

Expanding enterprise needs volunteers. Must be at least 18 years old, no upper age limit. Married couples eligible if both qualify and no dependents under 18. American citizens only.

Immediate opportunities for skilled craftsmen, librarians, home economists, farmers, nurses, surveyors, elementary & secondary school teachers, auto mechanics, pattern-makers, medical laboratory technicians, agronomists, and many other professions. To serve in poverty-stricken and disease-ridden areas of Africa, Asia, and Latin America—from Timbuktu to Katmandu. Tour of duty: two years. Motives necessary: to help others to help themselves while learning from them and about life in general. Status seekers need not apply. No company benefits. Living allowances provided for clothing, housing, medical care and incidentals. Must be willing to adjust radically to different way of living. Can you qualify? The opportunities are many and the need is great. For full details, contact the Peace Corps, Washington 25, D.C.

This appeal has never appeared in any newspaper, but it gives an idea of what is demanded by the Peace Corps. It also shows the problems faced by the new agency. Of all the tasks an organization has to tackle, the most difficult is recruiting the right people for the job. One misfit can undo years of painful planning and hard work.

This is especially true in selecting workers for service overseas. Faults that one's own countrymen might overlook become inexcusable among a sensitive foreign people. Eugene Burdick's *The Ugly American* was, if anything, an understatement of the dangers in this area. Consequently, regardless of how costly and involved an adequate process of rigid screening and selection may be, experts in the field—government and private enterprise alike —feel this is one place where cost must be ignored. The future of the Peace Corps will depend primarily on the success or failure of the first teams sent abroad.

The need for caution is a matter of concern for the foreign aid advocate as well as its foe. The Peace Corps should not be an escape for our often-cited "restless and purposeless youth." One United Nations technician summed up his doubts with this comment: "As I see it, these bumptious kids are an American problem; can't we solve it without bothering the rest of the world?" That this fear is widespread—and to a degree justified—was testified to by Jack Gould, television critic for *The New York Times:*

> Last night's television documentary "The Red and the Black" provided a strong argument against unleashing ill-prepared youngsters on an unsuspecting world. . . . The interviews were chilling in the extreme. Though their ostensible mission was to teach, not one of the young people could claim professional teaching experience. None had familiarity with the [host] language . . . in the arena of international affairs they were practically inarticulate. . . . The youngsters, whose chief qualifications seemed to be wholesomeness, good will, and energy, inevitably invited a conclusion that the underdeveloped countries had been made the latest stop for wide-eyed American tourists.[1]

The youths Gould spoke of were in Guinea as English teachers, and his complaint was supported by the Guinean Government. Three out of twenty American teachers sent to Guinea broke their two-year contracts and left the country after a few months; Guinean officials remarked bitterly that "the Americans could not take it here, our living conditions were not good enough for them." [2] If the Peace Corps, a U. S. Government agency, had sent these young teachers out, the venture would have been doomed even before it got on its feet, and the United States would have received a black eye in

[1] *The New York Times,* January 23, 1961.
[2] *Ibid.,* February 3, 1961.

the opinion of the world. Private foreign aid agencies emphasize, therefore, that none but the cream of the crop should be chosen.

CRITERIA FOR SELECTION

Personal Characteristics

Senator Humphrey's "Youth Peace Corps" bill set an age range of from twenty-one and a half to thirty-two years, and the opinion of the private agencies interviewed, with few exceptions, is that twenty-one to thirty is the ideal span. Under twenty-one, it is felt, the prospective worker has not had enough experience to give him a sufficient background; by twenty-one, a young man or woman should have experienced enough of life to be able to adjust to new situations. After the thirty- to thirty-two-year range, effectiveness usually lessens, both physically and psychologically. Also, a person above that age has trouble adjusting to teamwork among new people, especially when his fellow workers are youths in their early twenties or of a completely different generation. However, the age problem will ultimately depend on the type of work to be done; the American Friends Service Committee and Operation Crossroads-Africa have found that boys and girls eighteen to twenty-one can be used satisfactorily in work-camp operations overseas. The early Peace Corps *Fact Book* stated that volunteers would have a practical age range of from eighteen to forty-five, with older people serving mainly as instructors at training centers or as overseas supervisors. Actually, officials have now decided that there is no "average" or "best" age for the Peace Corps; it all depends on the job to be done.

Should women be sent overseas? With the so-called "weaker sex" accounting for more than one-third of all volunteers so far, the Peace Corps answers with an emphatic *yes*. Though early studies omitted women from consideration, the Peace Corps has found wide use for them as teachers, home economists, and so on. In fact, there are many situations in which a woman can do a better job than a man can do. In many Oriental countries where it is taboo for a woman to be treated by a male doctor or nurse, women have also been useful as instructors of home economics and other domestic arts. One of the basic problems overseas is diet. Occasionally, even where food is adequate, ignorance of food conservation and of how to prepare the simplest dishes results in a perpetual state of ill health for the Asian family.

A related problem is whether or not male and female volunteers should work in the same project. Many fear such a situation will result in failure because of the romantic temptations involved. However, both the Quakers and Operation Crossroads-Africa report that they have never had any great problem here. Stephen Carey says that, on the contrary, "Projects employing both men and women—especially if in a lonely outpost—are beneficial. Both morale and the tone of the work," he added, "are improved, without any unfortunate moral difficulties. The people we select have a firm religious background, and we have not had a single case of misbehavior. The only time when difficulties arose was when a boy and a girl on a project started going steady, and this partially disrupted the teamwork of the group. However, it only required adjustment by team members to the new situation, and happily this occurred." Mr. Carey continued by saying that the biggest problem of male and female volunteers is one of cross-cultural adjustment. Customs and dress in most countries are different from ours; girls in certain Latin-American and Oriental lands are not allowed to wear shorts or other abbreviated dress, and they must watch their step in their relationship with the local men. A situation that is considered innocent in the United States may, and often does, have very ugly connotations in Africa or Asia, for example.

Many married couples are joining the Peace Corps, and mid-1962 saw 135 couples serving overseas out of the total of nearly 3,000 volunteers. The policy is that they will be accepted only when both partners qualify, if there are no apparent marital problems, and if they have no dependents under eighteen years of age.

Similarly, several private volunteer agencies also require that married couples be married for a certain length of time. The reason is that they have had unfortunate experiences with couples who tended to use the work tour as a sort of prolonged honeymoon. One agency worker with years of experience added grimly that the "boondocks of Southeast Asia is not the best place for newlyweds to adjust to each other and to their new state of life."

With married couples the question arises as to what would happen if the wife were to become pregnant during the tour of duty. Professor Samuel P. Hayes of the University of Michigan has suggested that "assignments of those couples to whom this happens can be adapted to permit at least one of the couple to complete the full term of service, and perhaps to have at least part-time service from the other member." [3] Peace Corps officials consider this solution impractical, however, and the general rule is that the couple would have to return to the United States. The only mitigating circumstances would be that the couple were financially well-off or that their place of duty was in a city where adequate facilities were available. But even there it is felt that a dangerous precedent would be set by exception to the firmly established rules that no outside income be allowed and that the work of the team take precedence over all other considerations.

What Sort of Educational Background Is Desired?

The purpose of the Peace Corps is to provide "middle manpower" to underdeveloped nations that, on the one hand, receive the highly skilled technical assistance of AID and the United Na-

[3] *An International Peace Corps* (Washington, D.C.: Public Affairs Institute, 1961), p. 60.

tions for such projects as hydroelectric dams and steel factories, while having, on the other hand, a large surplus of unskilled labor. What they lack is the "middle" or semi-skilled techniques of basic industry, agriculture and other occupations.

For these reasons, AFL-CIO officials feel that volunteers experienced in a particular skill, yet having no more than a high school education, might be used. Many people, either lacking an aptitude for formal studies or forced to leave school for various reasons, know their trades—in many instances, skills that cannot be learned in colleges —from A to Z, and are of the opinion that they could contribute badly needed techniques to the new nations.

However, there is a ground swell of doubt concerning the use of anyone except college graduates. There are even some who feel that anyone going overseas to instruct ought to have at least a master's degree. The first reason for this is a belief that a college education is usually a broadening experience that cannot be gotten elsewhere.

In the second place, the Peace Corps, like the private agencies preceding it, will have to contend with the feelings of the host country. Many countries, it has been pointed out, may find it a bit insulting to be offered technicians with nothing more than high school diplomas, perhaps feeling that a non-college-educated volunteer is not the best to be had, as the Peace Corps advertises itself; the reasoning is, rightly or not, that if the person is so outstanding, why didn't he find some way to get his degree?

Many private agency officials feel that this is certainly true for the initial recruitment purposes of the Peace Corps, but that it is too parochial a view for the long run, now that the agency has begun to expand its activities to meet the needs of the underdeveloped countries. The official policy is that *all* qualified volunteers will be used, regardless of formal education or the lack of it. However, the statistics for the Peace Corps' first year in operation overwhelmingly favor college-educated volunteers, as noted in the chart below.

LEVEL OF EDUCATION
Total—2,816 Volunteers

HIGH SCHOOL	COLLEGE ATTENDED BUT NO DEGREE	BACHELOR OF ARTS/SCIENCES	MASTER'S DEGREE	DOCTORATE
120	730	1715	235	16
5%	23%	62%	9%	1%

Tied in with educational qualifications is the volunteer's knowledge of foreign languages. The International Voluntary Services and several other organizations do not require skill in the language of the host country, for the most part because such languages are "exotic" or little known. IVS has an intensive program of language study for the volunteer *after* he arrives at his post. Operation Crossroads-Africa, on the other hand, normally selects only those college students who are willing to add intensive language study to their normal work load *before* going to Africa. More important than an actual grasp of a particular language is skill in languages in general, or language aptitude. Service schools and certain universities have shown that a person with normal intelligence and some language aptitude can learn the basics of a particular language in as little as three to nine months of intensive training. The Peace Corps combines approaches of IVS and Operation Crossroads-Africa.

General Experience Background

The Peace Corpsman will not be expected to be a jack-of-all-trades, but neither should he or she live in a world bounded only by a chosen specialty. Most college volunteers will have had only summer or part-time work experience, and in this case the examiner must consider extracurricular activities. In this category, for example, are work with a Boy Scout troop, counselor in a summer camp, tinkering with automobiles as a hobby, or organizing a political or charity drive. When a companion of the late Mahatma Gandhi of India heard of the Peace Corps, she advised the United States to send youths who know how to laugh and make other people laugh. Asia, she said, knows enough of sadness so that there is no need for serious-faced boys and girls to teach more of it to her people. For this reason, although Peace Corps work will not be play, it is considered essential that volunteers know how to participate in games and how to dance, if only a few basic steps. Entertainment in very many other ways will be out of the question—there are no electrical outlets in the bush of Africa or the jungles of Southeast Asia for a stereo hi-fi set; as housing space is at a premium, books and magazines will be few. This is far afield from technical competence, but it is nonetheless important.

It is hoped that volunteers who have worked with private agencies or colleges in Peace Corps type operations will give their services to the new agency. Others considered valuable by the Peace Corps are people who have lived for a considerable time overseas, either as business representatives or armed forces dependents. Anyone who has had to adjust to a foreign culture will already have overcome the initial barrier, although different cultures raise different problems. Not so valuable are tourist trips of the ordinary sort; no tourist gains much more than a superficial insight into a foreign culture.

Personality

What are the personal qualities needed for success in overseas operations such as the Peace Corps? Harlan Cleveland decided that the five most relevant elements are: technical skill, belief in mission, cultural empathy, a sense for politics, and organizational ability.[4] The National Council of the Churches of Christ lists integrity of char-

[4] *The Overseas Americans* by H. Cleveland (New York: Mc-Graw-Hill, 1960), p. 263.

acter, a high sense of values, motivation for service, and willingness to do a hard job. The Quakers have similar standards: maturity, adaptability, religious motivation, ability to get along with others, ability to evaluate the total situation or perspective, and a sense of humor. However defined, they all add up to the secret ingredients that make for success. A volunteer is not expected to have all of them in the fullest degree, but he is expected to show that he possesses more of these qualities than would be needed to succeed at home.

Motivation and Ideals

All Peace Corpsmen will be expected to have a higher motive for service than the almighty dollar or love of adventure. What the private agencies have looked for in a recruit is a humanitarian zeal to help his fellow man, combined with a willingness to do a hard job. The pie-in-the-sky idealists are usually disillusioned soon after they arrive at their posts. Fighting mosquitoes in the middle of the night and working in swamp water up to your knees in mud is hardly a very glamorous aspect. Working with a peasant who is wondering where his next meal is coming from or trying to replace ancient attitudes of fatalism leaves no room for the anti-Communist crusader or the religious fanatic. But the cynic will be out of place, too. One has to have a pioneering spirit of some sort to maintain the spirit of enthusiasm needed in the face of frustration after frustration. Many volunteers make the mistake of thinking that they will see immediate

72

success in their particular project; on the contrary, it is all too often that the fruits of labor are only realized in an overseas project long after the technician has gone home.

A common motive for engaging in such work is an interest in broadening one's education and experience. The worker in Tanganyika should try to learn from the Tanganyikan culture, instead of going over just to teach others his own country's methods. A one-way exchange is no exchange at all, and this is part of the reason for the well-publicized failure of so many efforts to teach new techniques to ancient cultures. This tendency, as a whole, is called cultural empathy, for it is a sympathy with other cultures. The foreigner working in another land has to learn not to measure everything by his own or his country's standards, and he must also resist the ever-present temptation to compare the ideals of his own culture with the often harsh realities of another.

Maturity

Maturity, of course, combines all these considerations, but by maturity in specific is meant a considered and good judgment, thoughtfulness and consideration of others, a spirit of co-operation in working as a member of a team, and, one might add, tact, humility and patience. Many of these are qualities Americans are not noted for particularly, but they are qualities that must be had and be practiced. An insecure, argumentative and opinionated individual, well known for a back-slapping camaraderie, is the worst possible volunteer, although in many parts of the world he happens to be the American stereotype.

Tolerance

Tolerance is a part of getting along with others, and it cannot be overemphasized. If a volunteer goes overseas with prejudices on any grounds—racial, political, religious, national or class—he jeopardizes the entire operation, especially of a foreign-aid enterprise such as the Peace Corps. Many of the newer nations have deep dislikes and misconceptions of America. A few unfavorable reports of events in Little Rock, Arkansas, or Montgomery, Alabama, often are more persuasive than forty years of painstaking agency work. The Corpsman will have to fight his own natural inclinations and swallow his anger when he runs up against resentment and insult from those he has come to work with and assist.

Ingenuity

Very important is ingenuity. It is this aptitude that finds solutions to the vexing problems confronting the Corpsman. Something of the spirit in the belief that the impossible takes only a little longer to achieve than the difficult should belong to the overseas worker. Though he is an English language teacher in the bush of Africa, he must also know how to help repair a plow or perhaps use crude materials to fix a well. This is one of the reasons why the International Voluntary Services insist on recruits with rural backgrounds.

Loyalty and Security

The touchy question of Communist infiltration has been brought up persistently by critics and supporters alike. In the spring of 1961, the National Conference on Youth Service Abroad came out against either a security clearance or a loyalty oath for volunteers. The reason, they argued, is that Peace Corpsmen will not be political agents and therefore should make no affirmation of loyalty other than the standard passport requirements for Americans traveling abroad. Quaker officials fear that security checks will arouse the suspicions of neutralist nations that volunteers are actually undercover CIA agents.

Peace Corps Director Shriver gave the official view of this problem in two separate radio-television panel sessions. In the first,[5] his questioner was Republican Senator Hugh Scott of Pennsylvania:

SENATOR SCOTT: Will you have an FBI check [of the Corps applicant]?

MR. SHRIVER: We're working very closely with Mr. [J. Edgar] Hoover. . . . We're also working with the Civil Service Commission, and I can assure you and any of your correspondents . . . that every effort will be made to protect the

[5] *Your Senators Report,* broadcast jointly with Senator Joseph S. Clark over Pennsylvania radio and television stations, April 2, 1961.

Peace Corps against any infiltration by foreign groups of any kind.

SENATOR SCOTT: Does that mean that there will be an FBI clearance on all of these people?

MR. SHRIVER: That will be determined by the Director of the FBI, not by me.

SENATOR SCOTT: If not by the FBI, will there be some form of security clearance?

MR. SHRIVER: Definitely.

Later, a student on *Youth Wants to Know* [6] said that in view of the sophistication and thorough indoctrination of Communist agents, wasn't it possible that American youths might be influenced by them? Mr. Shriver answered with an emphatic no, and said:

You have to remember we're sending over people who are mature and well-balanced and well-trained, and they're under leadership that's going to be very able, so that when they're in a country, we will be seeing what they're doing . . . they know a lot about the United States. I'm not scared that they're going to be turned into Communists simply because they see a Communist. Perhaps they'll turn the Communists into Americans.

A few of the voluntary agencies have had close calls with Communist-oriented individuals. None, however, have slipped through their tightly controlled selection processes or, in the case of those

[6] WABC-TV, New York City, July 9, 1961.

having contracts with AID, through the government security investigations.

The experience of more than a year has convinced Peace Corps directors that a thorough security check on every applicant was too much of a strain on the FBI's limited resources. Now only cases termed doubtful by the Civil Service investigators are turned over to the FBI.

Selection of Leaders

Dr. J. S. Noffsinger of IVS called this the "great bottleneck." All of the private agencies insist that a team can be made up of outstanding rank-and-file volunteers, yet fall apart because it lacks proper leadership. On the other hand, an outstanding leader can take a bunch of raw, even mediocre, recruits and weld them into an effective work unit.

In 1960, Dr. Harold Isaacs of M.I.T.'s Center for International Studies surveyed the personnel problem on the spot for Operation Crossroads-Africa. In stark, realistic terms, his confidential report pinpointed many of the pitfalls that confront the Crossroaders—and the Peace Corps. He noted that there is no infallible litmus test for selecting the right leaders, but he said, "The evidence does suggest, however, that the better leader is more likely a man than a woman, a younger man rather than an older man, near enough in age [to the group] to pitch in with the work and enjoy the more active parts of the fun, yet old enough to be plainly senior to the young adults in his charge. . . . Who knows and likes young people . . . who knows how to be

77

careful without being overcautious, how to deal sensitively with individual needs and problems while respecting the needs of the group."

The petty tyrant, the study advised, is anathema. Group participants rated leaders "excellent" or "good" on the basis of how they combined democratic use of their authority with skill and common sense in dealing with unexpected and difficult situations. "The leader," Dr. Isaacs summed up, "should have the ultimate power of veto and decision, but he should operate in a way that requires him never to invoke it."

Just as important as his relation to the group is the leader's verve and sensitivity in getting to know the people of the host country and the tangibles and intangibles of any local situation. Many problems arise out of the difference between what people *say* and what they actually *do*. Americans, for example, are noted for their punctuality, so that around the world there are now *two* concepts of time instead of just one: American time and local time. If the leader doesn't understand what a problem is all about, then those in his command will almost certainly also fail. An overseas technician with more than forty-five years of field experience observed that village people are nobody's fools; they're keen judges of character and quickly separate the real from the phony. With a centuries-ingrained shrewdness, they have no qualms about exploiting a leaderless situation, especially where the leader—supposedly the spokesman of the group

—cannot give his workers an effective example of how to deal with their host counterparts.

Peace Corps standards are as rigid as, or more rigid than, those of the private agencies. In April, 1961, the newly born Peace Corps began a muffled "talent search" for overseas leaders. The job is rugged, to say the least. The 1962 Annual Report to Congress listed the following as musts:

First, the Peace Corps representative must have much the same motivation as the volunteers in order to provide the personal leadership necessary in a Peace Corps project.

Second, he must have had a successful career in the United States which he is willing to leave to serve in the Peace Corps.

Third, he must have the capacity to be responsible to the American Ambassador, serve as a mission director and at the same time seek his friends and associates outside the American community as well as within.

Fourth, he must forego all diplomatic privileges and immunities, except certain customs and tax exemptions, all hardship allowances, all PX privileges and live at a standard usually below that associated with the diplomatic community.

Fifth, he must have the diplomatic skills to deal with host governments even at the presidential and cabinet levels.

Sixth, he must have the administrative qualities needed for difficult and complex operations and the creative ability to make the most effective use of volunteers requested by the host government.

79

Seventh, he must know or learn the language of the country to which he is sent.

Eighth, he must exemplify, mentally and physically, the dynamic image of the United States.

A candidate meeting all these standards is personally interviewed by the Director, and his portfolio is then turned over to the Civil Service Commission for complete investigation.

The first "talent search" director was William Haddad, former New York *Post* reporter and now Associate Director for Planning and Evaluation. John D. Rockefeller IV presently serves as special assistant to Director Sargent Shriver in charge of the leadership search. Mr. Shriver has emphasized the importance of this particular selection process by noting that of the first 200 leader-candidates interviewed by him, only 11 met the requirements. And of the total interviewed to date, only 16 per cent have made the grade.

In light of the exhaustive nature of the selection process, skeptics find it difficult to believe that, for the modest financial rewards involved and the sacrifices demanded, many will want to apply. For young men, a further complication is the threat of the military draft upon completion of Peace Corps service. One Peace Corps official has said frankly that this unresolved question "will make my selection problem much simpler. Those who still have the motivation, the gumption, the adventuresomeness and the flexibility required will select themselves. They will see two or three years overseas helping others to help themselves as an opportunity not to be missed, as an addition to their own qualifications, not just as an interlude or a waste of time. I will still have thousands more applications than I can handle."

CHAPTER 2

WHAT SORT OF PREPARATION?

The Peace Corps will involve placing large numbers of Americans in day-to-day, person-to-person contact with the peoples of the underdeveloped nations. Too often in the past, however, many technicians have found themselves suddenly uprooted from the familiar surroundings of their native America and thrust into the midst of a foreign locale, ignorant of its culture and special problems. The reason is obvious: little or no advance training. This is true not only of American private enterprise operations overseas, but also of government programs. It was not until the Foreign Service Act of 1946 that any systematic training was provided the professional U. S. Foreign Service officer! It took two world wars and innumerable international conferences to get Congress—and public opinion—to recognize American involvement in the world arena as more than a temporary aberration.

The dangers of inadequate preparation for overseas work have tragic and comic aspects alike. Lee

St. Lawrence, advance scout for the first Peace Corps project, learned that lesson 250 miles back in the remote bush of Tanganyika. Tribesmen told him of a geologist who had been killed merely for breaking up some rocks. His crime was that he had failed to get permission first from the local chief.[1] On the more comic side, a Catholic priest tells this one on himself. Some years ago, newly assigned as a missionary, he joined villagers in hacking away at the jungle. He later noticed that, despite the blistering hot day, one young girl was putting in more than her share of the work, and he decided the only suitable recognition of such industry would be to invite her to dinner. That done, he was surprised no end when the girl's father grimly informed him that a wedding was in the offing for the two. It seems that, in that part of Africa, to invite a single girl to dinner is the same as a proposal of marriage. The priest wryly noted that it took some real talking to extricate himself from that situation!

Orientation

Strictly speaking, orientation and training are two separate phases of the preparation for overseas work. Orientation is concerned primarily with the culture of the host country, the history and special conditions in the surrounding area as a whole, United States history and public policy, and human relations. The goal of training, on the other hand,

[1] New York *Herald Tribune*, April 30, 1961.

is to provide or improve the various professional skills that the volunteer will need in his work, and to drill him intensively in the language of the country that he will serve and in general linguistic studies. The Peace Corps has integrated the two phases into a continuous training program.

Because most Americans on going to a so-called "exotic" land like Ghana or India will have either very little idea of what to expect or a lot of stereotyped misconceptions, it is obvious that orientation becomes a factor of the greatest importance. A newcomer is expected to commit the usual number of mistakes during his first two or three months on the scene, but it is hoped that a good stiff orientation will both lessen their harmful impact and familiarize the trainee enough to acquire before too long a time the *expertise* of an "old hand." However, as one IVS technician wrote recently, "Theory is of little value in working with peasant-type people. No amount of Stateside training will be of as much benefit," he said, "as on-the-job training, because to learn the feel of the country and how the people think, you must actually be there—not sitting in a classroom 3,000 miles away."

The majority of experts consulted for this study disagree with this judgment although they grant it a certain validity. One of the primary reasons is that here in the United States there are numerous facilities adequate for intensive Peace Corps training, whereas they are practically nonexistent in would-be host countries. According to the American Council on Education's survey of 468 colleges and universities, 43.5 per cent have special international programs available, while 61.7 per cent are prepared to accept Peace Corps contracts for training volunteers. Another reason why it would not be practical to omit orientation and training in the United States is the outcry it would arouse from both supporters and critics of the Peace Corps. It would merely confirm skeptics in their impression that the new agency is just another costly boondoggle which will cost us the respect of the world by sending over droves of naïve, untrained youths.

In actual practice, the Peace Corps has set up a tough training program. Although projects differ vastly and no two programs are alike, a typical course for volunteers includes eight major areas of study. The number of hours allotted to each part is based on a two-month program, having six-day weeks and ten-hour days.

1. *Area studies—65 hours*
   The history, culture and institutions of the host country within the framework of the surrounding region, as well as current events.
2. *Language—100 hours*
   Knowledge of the native language's structure, basic vocabulary, conversational practice, and technical terms for use in the project.
3. *Technical studies—100 hours*
   Knowledge and skills required to perform the assigned job in the overseas project.
4. *American studies and world affairs—50 to 75 hours*

United States history, culture and institutions. Contemporary world problems and the role of the United States on the world scene.

5. *Communism—20 hours*
The philosophy, strategy and tactics of Communism, and its role in contemporary world affairs.

6. *Peace Corps orientation—20 hours*
The mission of the Peace Corps and the volunteer's role within it.

7. *Health and medical training—30 hours*
First aid, personal hygiene, and preventive medicine.

8. *Physical training and recreation—60 hours*
Personal physical fitness. Instruction in American and host country games and folk dances.

Many volunteers, particularly those bound for Latin America, follow their Stateside training with a month at the Peace Corps Field Training Center in Puerto Rico, described in the Appendix to this chapter, then from one to two months of pre-project training in the host country.

The Host Country

Since people's reactions are determined largely by previous conditioning, a worker overseas must be aware that his activities are being thought of—judged, really—according to the standards of the country and the village where he is living. These are more often than not quite different from the standards to which Americans are accustomed. To know just what the local citizenry's impression is and what relationships with them really are, it is necessary to understand their viewpoint. The foreigner does not have to adopt that viewpoint, but his effectiveness depends on his being aware of it and sensitive to it. He cannot accomplish this unless he has studied the history which has conditioned the culture and the institutions of the people with whom he works. Neither can he understand their problems and the day-to-day events in their nation's life unless he first tries to place them within their own cultural context—not through the eyes of American culture, but instead by putting himself in their shoes and then asking himself how they would see it.

Much of the traditional pageantry and social customs in underdeveloped countries are colorful and fascinating to the foreign eye, but there are many others which are not. If the Peace Corpsman who goes to work in a country is largely ignorant of its less-attractive customs and the reasons behind them, he will soon leave in disgust and frustration. Dr. Noffsinger of IVS expressed particular concern about this problem. The impatient foreign technician, seeing the disease and poverty rampant in a country such as Egypt, for example, decides to solve these ancient curses of mankind with one fell swoop. "Aha," he says in effect to the Arab fellah, "I see people are dying like flies in this province from malaria. I'll get some DDT spray and kill the mosquitoes that spread it." The peasant just shrugs his shoulders and protests that nothing can be done about it, it is the will of Allah. The foreigner brushes his protest aside as superstition, takes his spray gun and eradicates the deadly malaria from the village. The people are healthy now, but, as Dr. Noffsinger pointed out, two problems have sprung up where once there was one. The peasant has lost both the moorings which were his faith and his confidence in himself, and his culture now has no meaning to him. Instead of feeling grateful to the foreign technician, he now resents him. The fast-moving world of modern technology has swept the underdeveloped peoples into a bewildering whirl-wind of change and into an awakening to the Darwin concept of "survival of the fittest." Some anthropologists feel that the angry nationalisms erupting in those nations are partly in reaction to the increasing displacement of the old values without replacing them with something equally strong.

Customs like this are not easy to change, and patience combined with understanding is the only answer. Prime Minister Jawaharlal Nehru of India has long butted his head against the granitelike problems of the caste system and overpopulation, and, it might seem, with little sign of accomplishment. His social workers have discovered after thirteen years in the field that these things cannot be changed overnight. And workers with the private voluntary agencies have often felt equally frustrated in trying to get vital projects off the ground, only to find themselves stymied by a notion universal among the less developed peoples—

the disdain of the educated elite for common labor and contact with the soil.

Forewarned is forearmed. By learning the obstacles ahead, the Peace Corpsman will realize all the sooner that it is only possible to attack them by approaching his work in an alien culture with the greatest degree of caution and tact.

Practical Living Conditions

Aside from cultural differences, there are equally practical, perhaps more down-to-earth, considerations. What kind of diet will the volunteer find in the area? How and where will he live? What community life can he look forward to? How sanitary are the people, and how is he expected to adapt to their habits? What medical care will be provided in case of illness or injury?

Most of these questions are answered adequately by case histories in Part III of this book, but an orientation program will have to answer them in detail, with a slant toward the locality where the volunteer will serve. An agricultural technician with the International Voluntary Services in Vietnam was asked recently what living conditions a Peace Corpsman might expect there. He wrote:

It has been the mistake of some to believe that you would live exactly as the local people do. If this were the case, most Peace Corps members would suffer from countless diseases. We most certainly do not have the same resistance as the people of the country. It would be foolish not to boil water and take other sanitary measures.

In my visits to tribal villages I eat rats, snakes or whatever they put before me; I drink rice wine and I sleep in a grass shack or in the middle of the jungle. I can assure you that it takes a certain amount of adjustment and that such an everyday pattern would be quite a strain. You can, however, live on the local level with some variation and improvement over the way the tribesmen do things, and by doing so, you can show them how to improve their way of life.

Despite such "concessions" as boiling water and putting up screens to ward off mosquitoes, Peace Corps Director Sargent Shriver was not overstating his point when he said that life in the armed forces may be more glamorous and much safer. Upon returning from an inspection of conditions in the West African Republic of Senegal, William Moyers advised Shriver in a memorandum to include a public sanitation expert and a health official with each Peace Corps team working there.

American Studies

In an earlier chapter, reference was made to criticism by Jack Gould, *The New York Times* television critic, that several overseas volunteers were practically ignorant of world affairs. Prior to the 1960 World Youth Festival, a non-Communist organization found itself confronted with a similar problem: the youths applying as American delegates to the Communist-sponsored affair had little or no background in United States history and current events. Past experiences at the 1957 Festival in Moscow resulted in a virtual rout for the unsophisticated few Americans who represented democratic opinion. Unprepared for serious debate and offset by numerous Communist-led delegates from the West, they were, for the most part, unable to give a persuasive defense of American institutions and policies. The clinching irony is that this was just a short time after the Russian suppression of Hungary's revolt, when the shoe should have been on the other foot.

It is inevitable that Peace Corpsmen will run up against barbed criticisms of America by hostile neutralists and professional agitators. There will also be honest, though no less loaded, questions by sincere and friendly hosts. Race riots in the Southern United States, the ill-fated Cuban invasion and the scandal of depressed West Virginia in our affluent country—these are only a few of the subjects American representatives encounter abroad. The Peace Corps has warned prospective recruits to expect a reception of this sort, but officials have warned the trainees that while they "will be expected to acquire background on political, economic, social, and religious institutions abroad (as well as those in the United States), they may not exhibit partisanship with respect to issues and organizations in these fields abroad." [2] Harlan Cleveland, the present Assistant Secretary of State for

[2] *Educational Institutions and the Peace Corps*, April 1, 1961.

International Organization Affairs and former dean of Syracuse University, has seemingly taken issue with this stand. Referring to the give and take of democratic debate within American society, he contends that representatives abroad should express their own mature views and, by doing so, "glory in our own pluralism." Sargent Shriver has scoffed at the fear that Corpsmen will parrot a predetermined government line, and he said that volunteers "no doubt will have to withstand Communist attacks . . . but we are not going over there to preach for a religion or a political system; we are going over there to work." [3] The Peace Corps' courses in contemporary affairs and their background are both comprehensive and intensive, so volunteers should hardly be at a loss for words in any debate.

Training

Of the 2,816 volunteers at work overseas or in training as of this writing, a wide variety of professional and technical skills turned up.

SKILLS	NUMBER [4]
Community development	120
Nurses	131
Public health	101
Medical laboratory technicians	43

[3] The Baltimore *Sun*, May 18, 1961.
[4] These figures include only those highly skilled and experienced in their work.

SKILLS	NUMBER
Home economists	61
Teachers	1,577
Vocational/manual	175
Arts and crafts	23
Engineers	51
Surveyors	39
Other	68

Language skills were also quite high. To qualify for fluency in a foreign language, a student should be able to do at least two of the following: give a short talk, read a newspaper, write a letter, understand a discussion. The requirements were met by a high percentage of students of five major European languages—French, German, Italian, Russian and Spanish—and there were many who were conversant with several of the so-called "exotic" tongues, such as Hindu, Urdu, Chinese and Arabic.

Obviously, most if not all of these skills will have to be adapted to the particular locale, as conditions often vary greatly from country to country and even within the country itself. The job to be done may require even further adaptation. For this, intensive classroom and work-experience training must be provided.

In addition, many volunteers, though adequately skilled in their specialties, lack the degree of proficiency needed in their overseas posts. An adequate training program has to tone up and develop the particular skill. The graduate of a liberal arts college who wants to teach English in a foreign country will undergo special courses in the English language and in teaching methods. If he speaks a language, he will have to study the local dialect to make any sense to his pupils.

The problem does not end there, however, and this is where *the* necessary ingredient comes into play. Call it ingenuity or problem solving, it all amounts to the same thing: common horse sense. A good illustration is this excerpt from the diary of a voluntary agency worker:

> When I first arrived in ——, I thought of myself as a teacher of English. But I soon learned other tasks were ahead for me.
>
> My school consisted of a small one-room hut. My heart sank when I looked in to find not a single desk or chair. The village elder, as if by way of explanation, told me that the building previously had been used as a storehouse for crops. Night was approaching, so I decided to just get a good night's sleep and worry about it tomorrow.
>
> The next morning, I assembled a squad of local men, and we went to work. With a few rusty tools and lots of elbow grease, we converted a few old citrus crates into halfway decent benches and a small lectern. A week later I was able to get hold of a sheet of tin and a bucket of black paint to improvise a blackboard. What tin and paint was left over I made into five small slates to give out as prizes for my harder-working pupils.

Since everyone was required to work in the fields in the afternoon, I could hold classes only a half day at a time. I soon found myself planting, plowing and carrying water from the nearby creek, when I wasn't grading papers and preparing my next day's lesson.

The tiny hut soon became too small for my students, who shyly trickled in, by twos and threes, from neighboring villages. I tried to hold classes out of doors, but the insects and the intermittent rain and hot sun discouraged that fast. The next time I visited the capital, I asked the USOM [5] if they could get an Ellston blockmaking machine for me. With that, a few bags of cement, some lime and the sand in the village, I soon had enough blocks to construct a 40 $\times$ 40 foot schoolhouse. I didn't know what accomplishment really meant until I walked in for classes the morning after and found the entire village assembled there to express their thanks.

Of course, not every Peace Corpsman is so mechanically inclined as to be a jack-of-all-trades in addition to his normal work. This is where a good training program steps in. Working with a common-sense individual, they can train him in job techniques by using simulated work situations in the classroom and in the field. That is why training sites such as our Indian reservations, the depressed areas and rugged camping trips have been used as part of the Stateside preparation for Peace Corps work. A volunteer should be taught

[5] United States Operations Mission.

the basic elements of gardening, home economics and personal hygiene, even if his main work isn't in that field. Why? In the first place, he may need them in his own day-to-day life, and secondly so that he can pass on some of this practical learning to his native counterpart or his pupils, as the case may be.

What about Language Studies?

Ever since the Russians fired Sputnik, the first space rocket, Americans have been concerned about their proficiency in foreign languages. Russian, which at the end of World War II was not widely taught, has now soared to one of the principal choices for study in universities and adult education programs. And some precocious tots in the primary grades are lisping *"nyet"* long before they have mastered Mother Goose rhymes.

Just how important *is* a foreign language? The overseasman, Harlan Cleveland believes, should study at least one language even if he can't master it.[6] The differences between cultures are so great that ignorance of a language often is a barrier to international understanding. The late President Franklin D. Roosevelt bemoaned this fact in speaking of his wartime relations with Russian dictator Joseph Stalin. "Unfortunately," he said, "the Marshal and I have no common language, and a shade

[6] *The Overseas Americans* by H. Cleveland (New York: McGraw-Hill, 1960), p. 263.

of meaning or an intonation is often lost, even through the best of interpreters." [7]

Sometimes, however, the language problem is overstated and gets woefully out of perspective. Mr. Cleveland came to this conclusion when he protested that language "ought to be viewed as an important subhead under cultural empathy, and our linguistic renaissance should not preclude our giving adequate educational attention to other elements of effective overseas performance." [8] No man should be sent to a hardship post like Senegal if he has a Ph.D. in French but none of the practical skills or the temperament needed.

Language training for Peace Corps work should be geared to the particular country or locality, but it should also be flexible enough to meet changing needs. Most experts are of the opinion that it should last from six weeks to six months, depending on the language itself and the individual's prior experience. The Army language school at The Presidium in Monterey, California, considers six months the necessary time to give an American an adequate command of a European language, but almost a year is required for Oriental languages. However, the needs of the Peace Corps are different from those of specialists in the armed forces, and this was clearly explained by Sargent

---

[7] Henry Field, "How F.D.R. Did His Homework," *Saturday Review,* July 8, 1961.

[8] *The Overseas Americans, ibid.*

Shriver, the Director of the Peace Corps, on a New York television panel: [9]

> QUESTION: Mr. Shriver, isn't it virtually impossible to learn a completely foreign tongue sufficiently in the normal training course of about six to eight weeks? And don't you feel that the whole training program is rushed a little too much for 100 per cent effectiveness?
>
> MR. SHRIVER: Well, in the first place, we're not trying to teach a whole foreign language in six to eight weeks. I agree with you, that's impossible. What we're attempting to do in two or three months in this country is to give the foundation so that you can learn the language successfully when you go abroad. Also, I would like you to know that in the foreign country—in each foreign country—there will be a training program in that country. For example, in Tanganyika, there's going to be a two-month training program for our people after they arrive, and during that time the training in the language—Swahili—will continue. So that, before our volunteers are actually at work in Tanganyika, they will have had three or four months of intensive training in the foreign language. We think this will be enough to make it useful for them and worth the effort that we put into it. . . .

Learning the language of your host has two values. First, its result will be the broadening of one's own experience and horizons, and secondly it expresses a certain respect for your foreign work-associate and his culture. Neutralist intellectuals who have toured the Soviet Union make much of the fact that the Russians have a special institution devoted solely to the cultures and languages of Africa. The United States cannot do less.

A training program is only as good as the people who staff it and the selection process which has preceded it. If both meet the rigid standards necessary for an overseas venture like the Peace Corps, then it can be considered adequate. In fact, leaders of the voluntary services are quick to stress that the training program should be regarded as part of the whole selection process, a trial period to precede actual acceptance into the Peace Corps. Sargent Shriver accepted their advice and has compared the new agency to a baseball team, with the manager always ready and able to yank out a player before he ruins the game. The fewer the misfits, the better the chances for the Peace Corps to succeed in its mission.

APPENDIX

TRAINING IN ENDURANCE

Many Peace Corps trainees undergo a grueling month of training in Puerto Rico before proceeding to the country in which they are to work. There the Peace Corps has set up Camps Crozier and Radley, twelve miles inland from the city of Arecibo. The site is 1,000 feet above sea level in a mountain range and a dense rain forest.

For Peace Corps officials, Arecibo has four basic advantages:

1. *Climate*—a taste of what to expect.
2. *Community development program*—Puerto Rico, under Commonwealth Governor Luis Muñoz Marín, has established rural improvement work in about 350 villages.
3. *"Spartan living"*—staff and volunteers sleep in tents, and only the minimum necessary equipment will be available.
4. *Foreign language and culture situation*—living and working among a people who speak a

101

different language and have different customs
and foods.

Round-the-clock is the order of the day. Peace
Corps officials emphasize, however, that theirs is
not a military type of "boot camp" training. What
they hope to develop in volunteers is an "inner
discipline" and sheer physical and mental endur-
ance. "The job," one instructor said, "is how to
make these fellows realize they've got more in
them than they ever dreamt. Of course, we have to
work on the assumption that these guys already
have something to start with."

And a tough program it is. Physical conditioning
plays a major part in toughening the trainees.
Under the general category of swimming are life-
saving and survival techniques. Here the volunteer
learns independence and confidence. Through
"drown-proofing," for example, his ability to overcome panic by cool thinking in a tight spot is
measured against the normal tendency to solve
problems of the sort by sheer force. This skill he
can later pass on to the people of the country
where he is to work. The value of such training
was put to the test in Nigeria, when a newly arrived Peace Corps volunteer saved the life of a
local lad by using "mouth-to-mouth" respiration—
this in spite of the fact the Nigerian had been
given up for dead.

Then there are the "rock-climbing" and aerial
obstacle courses, which involve scaling cliffs and
climbing ropes over rivers and chasms. Further-

more, while his own effort is essential to the success of his climbing, safety also depends upon a rope tied around his waist and held by another person above him (the belayer). He also takes his turn holding the safety of another person.

A four-day hike coupled with underwater swimming and descending from the Dos Bocas Dam on a rope combine to challenge the trainee to the utmost use of his skill. He has to rely on his personal command of Spanish and his ability in map and compass direction-finding—his new-found knowledge of tropical plants must procure most of his food during the trek. Volunteers are purposely cast in groups of ten in a situation where no one has been given responsibility or the labor divided—a natural leadership selection process.

Since many groups train in Puerto Rico during the hurricane season, their medical and survival training may come in handy. They are given first-aid situations. Experts then judge their reaction and their approach to the problem at hand. If a hurricane should hit the area, they will have to worry not only about their own survival, but also about the rescue of the local villagers. Shelters would have to be constructed, food provided, and first-aid and transport to nearby hospitals given to those caught by the storm. Woven throughout the entire experience is the idea of service to others, rather than self-preservation.

In addition to a continuous, though less intensive, course in the language of the country he will later serve, the volunteer has evening lectures covering three areas:

1. *"Critical incident."*
2. *Current events*—includes discussion of the civil rights problem in the United States, the Cuban invasion, the U-2 incident and other U. S. policy questions, as well as the Hungarian Revolution, the Pasternak affair, etc. The object, Peace Corps officials say, is not to "brainwash" those we send to work overseas but to make them aware of the several sides to each question, in case they get involved in similar discussions.
3. *Human relations*—differences in individual and group relationships in a foreign country.

Of the three, the "critical incident" is perhaps the most important. How is the Peace Corpsman to react in a delicate situation? For example, the Corpsman and his local work-associate might be sitting and talking in a local restaurant. In comes an American contractor, frustrated by his problems and tired from long days without sleep. He begins ranting and raving about everything in general and against local conditions in particular. The Corpsman tries without success to quiet him down or send him away; instead, he gets worse. Should the Corpsman try to pretend the embarrassing situation doesn't exist? Or does he grab the contractor by the collar and drag him out? This is just one type of question a Peace Corps volunteer will have to solve for himself.

Training in Puerto Rico does not involve only theory or experiment or physical fitness, however. Trainees spend from four to six days participating in community development projects, not in large groups but in pairs. Each pair is put aboard a *publico* (Puerto Rican bus) and goes to an assigned village. There they live with a Puerto Rican family and work in co-operation with and under the direction of a Puerto Rican community organizer. Whether they build pigsties or plan forest trails is up to the organizer. At times this training involves working in a city slum, rather than in rural areas.

The most serious casualties expected from such rigorous training are a case or two of dysentery, sprains or bruises, perhaps a broken bone—and a few trainees who are not able to make the grade. Its object, however, is to assure that the volunteer will not only have been trained technically, but that he will learn the real meaning and purpose of the Peace Corps.

PART THREE

CASE HISTORIES

OF PROJECTS

CHAPTER 1

IVS/INDOCHINA

The program that Peace Corps officials credit as a parent agency is the International Voluntary Services, which began in 1953 as the godchild of the late Secretary of State, John Foster Dulles. IVS works under contract with AID and several private foundations, and its technicians have served in countries of Africa, the Near East, and Southeast Asia.

To give an idea of what IVS men have been up against and of how they have gone about their tasks, this chapter is in the form of "newsletters" filed by a fictional IVS technician. The place is Lonkam, a mythical country somewhere in Southeast Asia, and the characters are all fictional. Though IVS/Indochina is a composite of several localities and projects, all incidents mentioned in the letters actually occurred—all were taken from actual field reports and newsletters on file with IVS, and nothing has been exaggerated. The fictional form of the chapter was taken at the request of IVS to avoid identification with particular projects or persons.

Ba-Vienh, Lonkam
September 6, 1959

DEAR FOLKS,

Hello from Ba-Vienh! Here's my first newsletter. I'd like to reply to each of you separately, but since that's out of the question IVS mimeographs copies for my friends.

Six weeks ago I was happily surprised to get a telegram from IVS headquarters in Washington saying "Join team at once in Kansas City. . . ." I had been dickering for several months with IVS to get the two-year assignment as an agricultural technician in Lonkam.

I threw my gear together in a hurry, said goodbye to all my friends in Milltown and took the bus to Kansas City. It still seems kind of strange leaving my farm in Kansas to take an unknown job halfway around the world. But I volunteered, and I'm thrilled by the prospects ahead.

After a couple of days of orientation, I headed for San Francisco. You might call 'Frisco the gateway between East and West: Chinatown, the old Spanish Mission Dolores, and the tall modern office buildings all blend in crazy-quilt fashion into a wonderful city.

From there we went to Honolulu, and spent a couple of days surf-riding and crammed in some more orientation. Then on to Tokyo, that half-

Westernized pearl of the East. As tourists, we heard the old story of the American woman who, when asked how she liked Tokyo, answered, "I don't really know. I went down to the Ginza once, but there were too many Japanese around." That takes the cake!

Our final stopover was Hong Kong. John Gordon, our chief-of-party, and his wife gave me a guided tour of the city. I ran through quite a few dollars in the process, this being the bargain capital of the world. But all of us felt guilty when we stared into the vacant faces of hungry refugees from Red China. Each day brings more of these pitiful people to this already overflowing tinderbox. Once-stout peasants from the southern provinces stand begging in the streets, rags clinging to their bones. The shacks, tenements and harbor junks that refugee families "live" in would arouse the most stonehearted of New York slum lords to reform.

By sunset we were heading back, weary and footsore, to our hotel, and then we sat around a pot of coffee and talked into the night of our experiences.

Transportation from Hong Kong to Lonkam is none too good. The plane we boarded early the next morning must have been a relic of one of Chennault's "Flying Tigers," and one passenger had a fit every time we hit an air pocket. None of us had any regrets when we stepped once again on the terra firma of Ba-Vienh, Lonkam's capital.

So here I am. In some ways now I almost feel

like a veteran, but I know I am the rankest of novices. It was several months ago that I began ransacking libraries at home for information on the tiny republic of Lonkam, located in Southeast Asia. Information was hard to find, but slowly it accumulated by bits and pieces. Now more than a month after leaving the States, I'm finding it almost as hard to find out how the Lonkamese mind works. Equally so is the task of dealing with the problems that arise in trying to bring modern techniques to an ancient nation whose customs are so different from ours. These are perhaps our greatest obstacles.

We've already run into a real juggernaut stemming from Lonkamese social customs. People here who are educated to any extent lose face if they do any work with their hands. On the other hand, it is nigh impossible for a man who works with his hands to get an education, regardless of his ability or talent. We need Lonkamese who are smart, who have some education, and who are willing to use their muscles.

Our two Lonkamese counterparts are very reluctant to discard hidebound norms enough to work side by side with us in manual tasks. How they expect to teach their countrymen how to assemble a plow, run an arc welder or stretch a fence, when they cannot bring themselves to dirty their hands to learn, is beyond me! If we do nothing more than put a slight dent in this crippling social custom during our time here, our mission will not have failed. Yet I cannot help but think that there must be many intelligent, dedicated young Lonka-mese who see the need to combine intellect with practical application—to stoop to conquer.

Here in Ba-Vienh the afternoon rains seem good to anyone who knows the droughts of our Midwest. This is the monsoon season. During this four-month period, nearly all of the annual precipitation is received—and that is over a hundred inches. A few days ago I went shopping without an umbrella. That was a mistake. With one along I could have walked home carrying the groceries—if I had rolled up my pants legs and carried my shoes at the same time. As it was, I took a bicycle taxi, called a *cyclo* here. It was slow but fun, like boating upstream. In many of the downtown "streets" the rainwater was up to the hubs of the bicycle wheels.

All in our team are from the Midwest or the South, and we have solid farming backgrounds. Three of us had our own farms and plan to return to them. This farm experience is a vital foundation for the work we're doing, and the degree I earned at Kansas State Agricultural College has come in handy as well. One reason we're here is our know-how of machinery, motors, crops and soils. But more important is the American willingness to work—a needed influence in a small Asian nation.

USOM (U. S. Operations Mission) has loaned our party quarters here in Ba-Vienh which we'll use while in the city for business or pleasure. Just when we'll get set up in the country we don't know yet. It looks like it will be Nam-Loq, a mountain town about fifty miles from here. We've already

113

done some "roughing it" at a couple of camps, but it is nothing like when we can set up our own station.

Today being Sunday, we went to church. Services are held in a large air-conditioned room in the Embassy which doubles as theater, meeting place, school for new arrivals, and recreation center. Space is at a premium.

Every day we study spoken Lonkamese and can boast a small vocabulary now. We can tell time, give directions, count, order a meal, and carry on a halfway decent conversation. Our tortured efforts are not wasted—Lonkamese are always telling us how impressed they are that rich Americans (*all* Americans are Rockefellers, we're assured) would take the trouble to learn their language.

Back in the States, you seldom got more than two lines out of me, but being in the boondocks has changed all that. Letters won't be too frequent, though, with so much to do and learn here. So long for now.

ANDY

Nam-Loq, Lonkam
November 2, 1959

DEAR FOLKS,

As I write this letter I'm sitting on a tree stump in our new camp. A foggy mist has hidden the neighboring peaks of the Rhadmer mountain range, and the sun shimmers through in quiet desperation.

For someone who enjoys the rugged life outdoors, this place is Utopia. Walking down a jungle bullock-cart road, machete in hand and a rifle slung over one shoulder, is just about the most enjoyable experience I've found yet. You can't see very far, but the forest sounds are there, and if you stop and really tune in, they can tell you a lot.

For the past few weeks we've been busy hacking away at the jungle, clearing a site for our temporary headquarters. Three pole-frame buildings, with thatched roofs and walls, have been built so far. Two of the largest are to serve as living quarters for the workers, and a small one will serve as an office of sorts.

Our own living quarters are rather unique. We have two large "covered wagons" in which we sleep on canvas cots covered with mosquito nets. Next to the wagons is a medical truck, complete with water-storage tanks, cupboards and an electric generator. Lonkam's Veterinary Service loaned it to us temporarily since it wasn't in use. Covering the whole arrangement is a thatched roof supported by a pole frame. And we have adequate pots and pans, dishes and utensils. For some time we had to make do with an old kerosene stove, but one of the workers' wives kept borrowing it and neglected to return it. So USOM recently contributed an old gas stove with an oven and a couple of bottles of gas. Our refrigerator is a hole in the ground in which we put a couple of ice chunks brought from nearby Nam-Loq. In short, all the comforts of home (well, almost).

A better setup is planned, but this will have to

do for the time being. We'll soon have to erect a makeshift shower. Until now, everyone has been bathing in the river. It's so muddy, though, that you have doubts whether the dirt is washed off, rearranged or just exchanged for more. The workers are no help at all in this respect. One of their practical jokers has been spreading rumors that a large crocodile occasionally visits our bathing area. Since we can't tell if this is just pure fantasy or some truth with the usual Lonkamese exaggeration, no one enters the water without getting jittery.

Working in the jungle is no unmixed pleasure, either. We have to wear clothing that protects our legs and feet from brambles, possible snakebite, and leeches. (The shorts worn in Hollywood movie scenes are only practical in clearings.) Leeches are a bloodsucker type of varmint found all over during the rainy season. Attaching themselves to your skin (legs and ankles mostly), they proceed to freeload on your blood to the bursting point, then drop off. The trouble is you ordinarily don't realize any of this until you look down at your blood-soaked pants or your boots start squishing. The ungrateful leech has an anti-coagulant effect, so the blood keeps flowing freely even after he's had his fill. This is dangerous only if large numbers of leeches join your little friend for lunch, or if the bite gets infected. It does seem a waste of good American blood, so we learn to tie our pants legs snugly and check occasionally.

The native workers we employ are a happy and

carefree lot. They have few worldly possessions, but apparently they're happy so long as they have a job, a roof over their heads, and ample food. Some are Moslem, others are Buddhist, and a minority are Confucianist. At one time, these groups formed distinct ethnic units because of their national origins, but the mixing of the races down through the years has made them practically indistinguishable in all but religion.

The personal friendships we are forming with the Lonkamese may be one important aspect of our work. They are finding that IVS team members are working people whose main interest is the projects underway. Living near the workers, taking the time necessary to help them learn new techniques, in turn learning some of their language and their ways of life, and in this way earning their respect as well as their friendship—these things we must and will do.

Of course, we neither pretend nor want to become integrated into Lonkamese society. Of necessity we are set apart from them—largely because of our different standards of living. But this can work to an advantage. Our tools and conveniences, few though they are in the field, are luxuries to the local people, and they attract their attention and fascination. This gives us a chance to apply a little basic mechanical education for the interested and ambitious ones.

By its very nature, our work is slow: success may come slowly, or even go unnoticed. Frankly, mistakes will be common and the alternative courses of action many. Because Nam-Loq Agricultural Station belongs to Lonkam's government, we, as part of the U. S. co-operative assistant program, must assume a backstairs role—not intruding, but rather willing to help where help is asked. Sure, we get discouraged sometimes—and confused. It's no easy matter to adjust to the shock of a new culture, to have all your old ground swept right from under you. But we feel this type of grass-roots, person-to-person effort is both vital and desirable. Our small-scale projects, coupled with the huge enterprises ICA has undertaken, can help to accelerate economic growth and to raise the living standards and human dignity of the individual Lonkamese as well.

We've heard rumors recently that Communist-supported guerrillas are pushing south, and we may hear from them yet. Repeated efforts by the central government to dislodge them from their mountain strongholds have largely been unsuccessful. Small wonder—that vast, uncharted jungle gives rebels (and bandits) ideal cover for strike-and-retreat operations, and after ten years in that maze, those boys are real experts in the arts of survival.

What do we do for entertainment out here, you ask. Well, the Lonkamese workers sit around campfires and tell tales on through the night. We don't understand much Lonkamese yet, but from the loud guffaws we hear, they must be humdingers. And every Wednesday night USOM supplies us with a couple of Lonkamese-language films. No English subtitles, but most of the films are travelogs and newsreels, and the scenery is often breathtaking. Have you ever seen the majestic waterfalls and rapids of Southeast Asia or the inside of ancient jeweled temples? And other films have featured the growth of the American Union. For many Lonkamese, these are the first movies they've ever seen, and they come for miles around. Incidentally, the spirit of free enterprise is no U. S. prerogative—the local women have a pretty good racket working on movie nights. These sharp operators bring in fruits, meats, and cooked rice to sell to the crowds at a nice profit.

Last week I got a touch of dysentery; I'm still a little woozy but otherwise okay. Our only accident happened about two weeks ago when a local counterpart, Dao Nonkin, was burned rather badly while lighting a pile of stumps and refuse. He's in the hospital at Ba-Vienh, but the way he's recuperating, he should be back on the job next month. He lost his eyebrows and eyelashes, and the skin on his face still looks raw, but the medic says it'll all heal up.

It's a damn good feeling to know that the French hospital in Ba-Vienh is good, both in facilities and staff. If need be, the USOM planes can fly seriously injured or sick persons at a moment's notice to the big hospital in Bangkok (Thailand). We have a dry landing strip at Nam-Loq, and USOM is going to install a telephone for use in emergencies.

Last night we had a real bull session via interpreter with our Lonkamese co-workers, and questions mostly concerned—yep, you guessed it—Little

119

Rock, the Cuban revolution, our two-party system, and the Cold War. Here the clash of ideologies is close to home, and there's no escaping it. We often meet Russian technicians and Chinese exchange students on the streets of Ba-Vienh, and sometimes out in the jungle country. Oh, they're very correct and polite, but there's no love lost. You realize increasingly you're being watched very closely, and your conduct is under strict scrutiny all the time. If you don't watch your P's and Q's, brother, you've had it. The fewer "ugly Americans" we get out here the better.

Well, take it easy, and drop me a line once in a while.

ANDY

Nam-Loq, Lonkam
December 28, 1959

DEAR FOLKS,

All your letters have now arrived. Such a wealth of news I've never seen: marriages and births appear the sole occupation of Kansans. If there is any single woman around, you might do me the favor of locking her in a cage until I return, because at this rate there won't be one left for at least the next couple of generations.

The life here, though never quite humdrum, is more natural to me now. I've found it is far easier to adapt the body to changes than it is the mind. My bony frame will readily welcome the hardest rock as a Simmons mattress, but making my mind go along is a different matter. The secret to meeting these difficulties is making mind and body achieve a balance in regard to all the aspects of the problem. Once you do that, you're okay. I admit that at the beginning I kind of worried whether or not I'd meet the requirements—now I laugh when I think of these early apprehensions.

We've learned that to get the work done around here you've got to work hand-in-hand with the people—it can't be any sham where the Americans walk in and take over, leaving the natives a few empty titles. My efforts with the Dalat tribes show this. The Dalat are hillbillies who live much as the American Indians in the frontier days.

About two months ago the Communists started pressuring the mountaineers into coming over to their side. The main basis for their campaign was that the government and the American "interlopers" had done nothing but give phony promises to "better the lot" of the Dalat. Sadly enough this was true in some instances, and the Communists were making headway in most tribal areas.

At the same time the Reds were pushing their effort, IVS/Nam-Loq was using every possible means to establish a basis of mutual trust with the Dalat. Meetings were organized with village leaders to discuss problems and the ways to solve them. Meanwhile, we contacted Lonkamese officials who might be of assistance if some means were found to offer a solution to the Dalat's problems.

However, a quick source of money had to be found. Our need was now, and confidence would have been lost had we been forced to wait on the usual "red-tape" government channels. But we were lucky in this case, as we got some funds right away from a private aid foundation.

A committee of Dalat representatives discussed with us the chances for an agricultural training school to learn techniques to better their lot. Lonkam's Minister of Agriculture promised full co-operation and the aid foundation approved our project on the spot. It was only a matter of days before the school was organized and in session. Arrangements were made for practical assistance such as seeds and plows. If projects like these can be carried out, they may be the very thing to keep Lonkam independent and free. Not so meaningful to the ordinary Lonkamese are the big money programs written up on paper to take place one or two years from now.

We had a visit the other day from USOM forester Jack Clark and a crew of laborers. They're surveying the jungles of the Rhadmer mountain ranges. The area is a large one. First you travel by jeep, then by oxcart, and finally by foot, often in places where no man has ever trod. There's one advantage, though: you automatically have a hunting trip at the same time.

Speaking of hunting, the local villagers are always warning us of the "Tiger Phantom." The legend goes like this. A hunter builds his perch in a tree near an animal that the tiger has killed and partly eaten. He sits there with his rifle and waits for the tiger to return for another meal. But the tiger is too smart. Realizing its foe is waiting to pounce, it takes the form of a most beautiful and seductive woman. "She" then lures the hunter from the tree for a *tête-à-tête.* Once he is on the ground, the phantom immediately changes back into a tiger and devours the hunter. The area abounds in rich folklore like this.

Mr. Noffsinger [1] in Washington was right when he warned us that we would need three indispensable things for success: patience, more patience, and still more patience. Nam-Loq's main occupation now is waiting—waiting for the local people to be paid for the land they have cleared so we can make it into fields, then prepare it for planting crops at the beginning of the rainy season; waiting for the road from the highway to the farm to be rebuilt, so that materials may be hauled in and out; waiting for permanent buildings to be built so that all of us—IVS staff, the Lonkamese counterparts, the equipment, and the livestock—will have suitable housing. And, of course, these are all major items which will be "started any day now" for the last month and more, that is, according to those responsible for getting the projects underway.

The river, translated, is called "the river which runs backwards," and now it's flowing toward the ocean like a good river should. I was a mite skeptical when I first arrived here when they told me it ran one way in the rainy season, then another during the dry season. The change in this ornery river has convinced me, though—the water level has

[1] Dr. J. S. Noffsinger, former chief of the International Voluntary Services; now a special consultant to the Peace Corps.

varied by as much as thirty feet from one season to the next.

Our native interpreter is also a professional fisherman. So he is leading the workers in construction of a fish trap. It stretches across the river to a point just above our swimming hole. We hope it will furnish enough fish for everybody. The trap, made of bamboo and vine, is designed to catch all of the larger fish which attempt to travel through it. The Lonkamese have warned our Chinese-born Izaak Walton that such a large-scale project could cause him bad luck with the river spirits. Maybe they regard such thoroughgoing fish traps as too greedy?

People in America can never realize the conditions that many people in Southeast Asia must endure. What is astounding is their attitude. Normal conditions at their best would be very uncomfortable for us, and at their worst a catastrophe. We live under the relative security of a strong government and a comfortably high standard of living; here the only government they understand is the village chief, and routine existence is plodding behind a water buffalo pulling a wooden plow in a soggy rice paddy. A robbery in the neighborhood is horrible to Americans; to Lonkamese this is nothing. The Red guerrillas attack their villages and then tell the survivors to pay their meager year's food-stores as tribute. The next thing they know the central government is on their backs with penalties for "collaborating" with the rebels.

Coexistence with tragedy and continual disquiet is the philosophy. One of the workers lost a month's wages and some clothing to a thief recently. I heard about it and went to console him, expecting to find him downcast and sullen. Instead, he was working furiously and smiled to me in greeting. When I asked him about his loss, he merely shrugged. "It could have been worse," he said. "Three days ago I had six months' pay saved, which I used to buy a rice paddy and that healthy buffalo you see over there. I'm glad the thief didn't rob me then." This looking at the bright side of things is a trait I envy. It's a native asset we couldn't do without in trying to do the impossible out here.

Otherwise, the weather has been dandy. We've forgotten what the long hard winters back in the States are like. Right now it's 92° F. in the shade. I felt kind of silly singing "Jingle Bells" Christmas Eve when it was like a day in mid-June.

ANDY

Nam-Loq, Lonkam
February 10, 1960

DEAR FOLKS,

The last few weeks have been eventful ones for us, beginning with the National Agricultural Exposition in Ba-Vienh. IVS played only a small part, primarily in preparing some of the Lonkamese Veterinary Service displays. Dr. Pham Ngao of the Service was over-all chairman of the fair, and Bill Pearce, our USOM adviser, gave us a great deal of assistance.

The Chinese Communists attracted a lot of attention with their textile loom, operating almost continuously throughout. Models of the textile mill, paper plant and cement factory—all completed and working—were large and appeared well laid out and equipped. Two of their industrial plants are near Nam-Loq, and together with the large modern Russian-built hospital in Ba-Vienh, make an impressive showcase of Communist aid in this area.

With complete modesty, however, we can say that the Veterinary Service display was the biggest hit of the fair. Peasants and foreign envoys alike craned their necks to see our exhibit: an incubator in which baby chicks were hatching. There were startled cries of glee as little bundles of fuzz began to pop out of their shells. In addition, Dao Nonkin, a Lonkamese counterpart, helped prepare a scale model of the livestock-development farm on which we are working; he set up buildings, fences, green grass and even cattle in the pastures. The farm model looked fine, and with the southern end of the mountain range for backdrop, the real thing should look even better.

IVS/Nam-Loq has undergone something of a revolution since my last letter. Enough progress has been made so that the remaining work of getting established can be laid out and checked off, item by item. Essentially all the temporary hourly workers have been laid off and sent to help other projects. All future work will be by contract. We hope to get more done for your money by paying for work *done,* instead of for the number of hours put in.

The right-of-way is being widened and cleared along the road from the highway to the farm. It is to be hard surfaced all the way in. The first few parts near the highway have been built up and prepared for surfacing, but the rainy season has arrived and the roadwork is only beginning.

Work in the plant nursery so far indicates that several local grasses will do well here. Also, millets, cowpeas, sorghums, legumes, and grasses from the southern part of the U. S. have done well during the dry season under irrigation. What they will do during the rainy season remains to be seen. The soil here is not fertile, even that which has never been farmed. Apparently the heat and the heavy rainfall decompose and leach organic matter and minerals from the soil at a very rapid rate.

The other day we were working out in the hot midday sun, and thought we would stop for lunch. That had to be postponed, however, while the mountain folk gathered around to stare unabashed at us newcomers, especially at the white woman (John Gordon's wife). This sport of staring is widespread all over Asia and just about everybody but the most sheltered prude gets a kick out of it. These people don't see too much of strangers, so after a while you get a little used to it. To sort of clear the air, we gave out with our best "hellos" in Lonkamese, though I'm sure they got an even bigger kick out of that.

Land clearing is progressing. All sorts of vegetables have been added to our diet: onions, radishes, cabbage, okra, and sweet corn. Six bulls have arrived from the States, and we've taught the farm hands how to teach them to lead and how to care for them. Another stroke of luck: USOM gave us a dilapidated but still quite workable station wagon for the long trips we must make. Hundreds of loads of sand have been hauled past our camp by trucks from the Red Chinese-built cement plant nearby.

Dao Nonkin has been in charge of surveying the 120 hectares that we'll have as extra pasture and crop land. Many trees, brush piles, and termite mounds have combined with intense heat to make progress slow. Still, more than half the area is surveyed now and drainage ditches can be located properly.

Our experimental plantings of Kenaf, a fiber crop, are the first in this area. We have hopes that it will be a new cash crop for the farmers here. By the way, the expanding industrialization of Japan is providing quite a market for fiber crops in the Far East.

The well has been completed and is functioning right. But it appears that we will have quite a time convincing the workers that they should not take baths, wash their clothes and dishes, etc., right at the pump. They are used to using water wherever they find it and see no harm in using all the water right at the pump where it's handy. No doubt they think we're nuts for insisting that they take their baths elsewhere.

Our project has at last passed through the embryonic stage successfully and is now on its feet. It's growing pretty fast. It shouldn't be too many months before we start "phasing out" and leave Nam-Loq in the hands of the natives we've worked with and trained. It's a weird feeling to work yourself out of a job—and then have to like it, too. But that's our mission.

ANDY

CHAPTER 2

CRS/HONAI (VIETNAM)

Catholic Relief Services, an agency of the National Catholic Welfare Conference, has been operating assistance programs since the late thirties, when it began resettling refugees from Nazi Germany. Since that time, CRS activities have expanded to many times its original effort.

The Peace Corps does not anticipate any health projects using skilled medical technicians; instead it will work with public health units designed to teach sanitation and to apply minor medical care. Doctors do accompany most Peace Corps projects, but their main job is the care of the volunteers. However, during the time he is not busy with them, the physician is expected to engage in voluntary service in the host country's health program; this is to compensate the country for any burden placed upon its limited medical resources by the volunteers. Still, the following CRS case history is important: The Honai eye clinic was very similar in circumstances and purpose to the work in Laos of the late Dr. Tom Dooley, whose example caused popular interest in setting up the Peace Corps.

Beginning in 1954, 900,000 Vietnamese "voted with their feet"—to use a pet expression of Vladimir Ilyich Lenin—in an election that had far-reaching consequences. The demigod of Communism would have been heartsick to see these men, women, and children fleeing his disciples' "People's Democracy" in North Vietnam for life in the bourgeois South.

The mass exodus conferred problems as well as a boon on South Vietnam. Many of the refugees were disease-ridden, and the war-torn nation had few facilities and still fewer personnel to handle even the most serious cases.

The most crippling of all is trachoma, the greatest single chronic eye problem in the country. In trachoma, the eyelids become deformed in such a way that the eyelashes scratch the cornea each time the individual opens or closes his eyes. It is not hard to see why it is painful, ultimately blinding and economically disastrous. Yet it can be cleared away in the early stages with simple drug treatment; in advanced cases, a minor operation will suffice. Trachoma victims can be rehabilitated in a matter of a week or so, as compared to the years-long treatment required for such Asian commonplaces as leprosy and tuberculosis.

Nearly as common are such eye afflictions as glaucoma, both local and virulent tumors, ulcer of the cornea, crossed eyes, and the ordinary "pink

131

eye." The trouble is that there are not more than nine eye specialists to care for the approximately 12 million Vietnamese.

In 1959, a concerned Hawaiian ophthalmologist, Dr. William Holmes, asked Catholic Relief Services to give an eye clinic project a trial run in South Vietnam. Monsignor Joseph J. Harnett agreed to sponsor it, and Dr. Holmes scouted around for qualified volunteers.

The site chosen was Honai, thirty kilometers from the capital Saigon. The Canadian nursing Brothers of St. John of God, themselves refugees from the North, staff a hospital there. American pharmaceutical companies and volunteer groups donated special medicines, drugs and equipment, while the German Bishops' Overseas Relief (MISEREOR) provided an X-ray laboratory. All these materials were shipped by CRS under the ICA ocean freight subsidy and were allowed duty-free entry by the South Vietnam government.

The volunteer eye specialists paid out of their own pockets for the transportation to and from Saigon. And for the duration of the project, they sacrificed their private practice back home. CRS provided the doctors with housing, board and transportation within Vietnam.

The makeshift character of the Honai clinic is emphasized by the fact that operating-room linens and surgical gowns were improvised from discarded surplus flour sacks and odd scraps of cloth. Used glasses were obtained from "Eyes for the Needy," an American organization; the greatest use of these was for those who have difficulty in using their eyes for near work.

By February, 1960, the project was off and running. The first ophthalmologist to report for duty was Dr. Eliot B. Hague of Buffalo, New York, who brought along his wife, a registered nurse experienced in eye work. After him came Dr. Jou S. Tchao of Lewiston, Maine, and Dr. Herman A. Iverson of Eureka, California. All were Protestants. Assisting the doctors were Brother Bernard Samuel and Mrs. Catherine Varella, a CRS registered nurse, plus the native staff of trainees.

Although the clinic was not advertised in the local newspapers, word-of-mouth and immediate results brought an onrush of would-be patients. Many traveled by foot from as far away as the town of Hué, 690 miles to the northeast. For this reason, in-patient facilities had to be enlarged several times, and when space ran out, patients were packed in the already-crowded wards. Patients able to take care of themselves were put in one big ward. At one time as many as 34 eye cases were cared for in one day at the hospital.

In the operating room, standards were made as close to Stateside hospitals as possible. What would have meant extra cost was accomplished through a lot of extra effort and longer hours. Scarcity of things that could not have been done without elsewhere would have created the same problem at Honai except that Asians toughened by hard life offered an incredibly high resistance to pain and suffering. Many patients went through as painful

133

a procedure as the removal of an eye with only a small dose of local anesthetic, gritting of teeth, and, as one remarked wryly, "much prayer." In the four months that the clinic was in operation, surgery on 389 cases was completed. Many more could have been operated on if another surgeon had been there to assume post-operative care and follow-up.

More than eye troubles were cured. Trachoma and similar diseases work havoc on human dignity. Unable to work or to lead a normal life, the victim often becomes morose, his spirits take a nosedive and his physical bearing is stooped. One young woman patient had been blind for twelve years. She had lost her right eye, and her left one had begun to fade away. Her daughter led her to the clinic, as she could not walk by herself. The operation was successful, and when her daughter returned to help her, she refused and walked unaided and standing straight, enjoying her newly regained self-reliance.

Of the thousands who came, a large number of all but the most serious cases had to be turned away. Even so, approximately 3,000 were examined and treated. The harassed doctors were, therefore, quick to see the need for an educational campaign to prevent or reduce advanced cases. Aside from the shortage of personnel, ignorance and reluctance to see a doctor cause most of the eye trouble in Vietnam. The hospital staff hung crudely drawn pictures on the walls, and attached some explanations in Vietnamese. Madison Avenue admen are not likely to award the effort the

Advertising Council prize of the year, but it went a long way toward accomplishing its purpose. Honai was helped here to a large degree by native medical authorities; Dr. Nguyen-Dinh-Cat, chairman of the Saigon University Medical School, supplemented their efforts by lectures.

One of the most pressing problems at Honai—and throughout Southeast Asia—was lack of qualified nurses and interns. The eye clinic tried to "steal" some help from the hospital, but they were so shorthanded that none could be spared. The lucrative fees that American medical technicians command make service in a project of this sort no small sacrifice, and it was recommended that CRS recruit personnel instead from Japan or Germany.

All reports to CRS have emphasized that the clinic should be put on a more permanent basis. But it is only during the four or five months of the dry season, from December to May, that work can be practical. In the monsoon, rice fields and harvesting occupy the undivided attention of the Vietnamese farmers; the rainy season imposes additional hardships on the needy and their companions who have to travel miles over the countryside to reach the hospital.

However, the Peace Corps feels that a permanently staffed hospital is out of their line. Realizing this, CRS has suggested instead a mobile unit which would operate throughout the area and close down when work became impractical or need not so immediate. Because of the policy barring contracts with religious agencies, CRS will not be assigned Peace Corps work overseas. However, neither CRS nor the Peace Corps disagree over the pressing need for a concerted effort to improve the abysmal health conditions of the Asian peasant.

B. The Peace Corps at Work

Within approximately six months after the fall of 1961, the Peace Corps sent into the field nearly 1,100 volunteers to start work in more than a dozen countries, with many more in training for nearly 100 projects.

The Peace Corps has followed the lead of the International Voluntary Services and other private agencies by encouraging detailed, folksy letters from Corpsmen at work overseas. The best of them are published in the two house organs, *The Volunteer* and the *Peace Corps News*.

In addition to being good public relations, these letters serve as indicators of project progress and of the adjustment of the volunteers to sharply different conditions overseas. At Peace Corps headquarters, they are studied for telltale signs of developments to be corrected or commended.

Following are examples of the better letters from volunteers in East Pakistan and the Philippines.

East Pakistan

Twenty-nine of us landed at Dacca airport on October 28, after flying 22 hours from New York via London, Frankfurt, Vienna, Beirut, Istanbul, Karachi and Calcutta. We stopped only to refuel;

I remember moving my watch ahead continually and being served yet another meal.

The group divided then; my half remaining in Dacca to live with Pakistani families and to attend language classes, while the others went 50 miles east to Comilla for more intensified classes at the Academy for Village Development. This first stage lasted about four weeks and was an excellent introduction to the people, daily life, food and Bengali. The latter is coming along slowly now, but for a while, I had serious doubts that I would ever understand anyone.

I lived with the family of Dr. Mojissundi Ahmed, a professor of chemistry at Dacca University. He is traveling now in the United States so we were a household of women: Mrs. Ahmed, their three daughters and me. They were a great help to me and getting to know each other was an experience for us all. They and their friends are as interested in America as I am in Pakistan. Many evenings passed comparing notes on what was done where. Mrs. Ahmed and I went so far as to bake an American-style apple pie in a Pakistani-style kitchen, without an oven. It wasn't bad, considering. And the children taught me Bengali script from a first-grade reader.

At the end of November we switched places with the other half of our group and spent three weeks in Comilla. Sponsored by the Ford Foundation in conjunction with Michigan State University, the Academy of Village Development has become one of the government's greatest hopes in improving agricultural techniques, developing co-operative associations, and raising the living standard of the villagers. The problems are numerous and complex, but we were impressed with the progress that can be made on a modest and realistic scale.

We made field trips to the surrounding villages, saw how life has been carried on for the past several hundred years—where often the rice crop is insufficient to feed the family, let alone provide profit for a year's work. We were a novelty to these people; the entire village gathered around us, friendly and curious and surprised that we spoke even a little Bengali with them. Women were absent from view; purdah—seclusion in the home as observed in Muslim countries—is still very much the practice. . . . They were amazed: why weren't we married, where was our jewelry, didn't our hair grow, and why didn't we put coconut oil on it?

There is beauty here, especially at day's end. Twilight is short and often spectacular; we have watched the sun drop quickly over the rice paddies and behind the coconut trees by the river. A complete lack of commercialism in the countryside sometimes makes it seem impossible that it's the 20th Century: multi-divided flat fields (green when we came, now parched in the dry season), dotted with small thatch-roofed villages, and roads traveled by foot or oxcart.

. . . In Comilla, Bob Burns has been placed in charge of the Academy's important irrigation program. Bob and his co-workers hope to double production on land that has historically been dependent on the monsoon for a single annual crop. . . . Bob Taylor has invented an inexpensive machine for parboiling rice, utilizing the rice husks for fuel. Parboiled rice is easier to husk and more profitable in the market, but the problem has been a lack of fuel for heating the water. Bob's machine blows the husks over charcoal, where they burn in mid-air, supplying the intense heat necessary to boil the rice.

Lloyd Goodson is responsible for keeping the Academy's twenty tractors running. On his second day on the job, a tractor rolled over an embankment while plowing. Lloyd carried the unconscious driver back, put him in his own bed for the night and early the next morning came out with a new tractor to right the one that had overturned. The Director of the Academy particularly appreciated this because, had the truck been allowed to lie in the field all morning, word would have spread throughout the village that "the Academy's tractors lie mostly on their sides with their wheels in the air."

RACHEL SCHAUFFLER

Seven weeks after our arrival in East Pakistan, we had completed our training and were ready to move to our jobs.

One group, considered the lucky ones at the time, remained in Comilla to work at the Academy. There, the engineers, youth workers, librarian, mechanic, farmer and photographer all have their work cut out for them. The eight-hour day and five-day week are luxuries not yet available at the Academy, but the satisfactions that come from seeing the fruits of hard work are plentiful.

In Dacca, the physical education teachers just about got their program into full swing when the university closed for Ramzan, the religious season. They're now en route to Comilla to help in setting up youth groups until the university reopens. One of the engineers who is teaching at the polytechnical school has moved from the Peace Corps house to the school's hostel and is managing to keep moving at least 12 hours a day. The audio-visual team at Dacca hasn't been sleeping either; one member went on a scientific expedition to St. Martin's island in the Bay of Bengal recently, while the other set up a display of audio-visual techniques at the East Pakistan Education Week Exhibition.

In Rajshahi, the teachers were managing to keep busy with their classes, planning for new courses and expanding the curricula of departments, a time-consuming and difficult task. One engineer is becoming proficient in Bengali, since he's using it rather than English as the medium of instruction. Another has just taken on the position of District Engineer of Rajshahi. At the Medical College Hospital, one of the girls is setting up a medical records section as well as assisting in the operating. Another nurse has persuaded her colleagues to sterilize the needles between injections and has established a system of medicine charts to facilitate dispensation of drugs.

In Mirpur, the two mechanics have just received a large mobile workshop from the Government of East Pakistan, and are kept busy maintaining the equipment of the refugee satellite towns of Mirpur and Mohamedpur. The carpenters are introducing pre-built doors and window frames that can be assembled at one place and then brought to the house building areas. Formerly, each window and door was built separately as each house was built, making standardization practically impossible. The mason has been experimenting with a new brick-making machine, bamboo-reinforced concrete walls, and is now starting his second building where he gives on-the-job training to new Pakistani masons. The Mirpur group recently lost one of its members when the town planner moved to become District Engineer of Pabna. The sociologist is preparing a census-sociological-medical survey which will be used in evaluating the populations of refugee towns.

The mason, by the way, had an experience that we won't let him forget for a while. He saw some other masons and hod-carriers busily working and thought he would give them a hand. He hopped over the wall that separated them from the street and began to help them, talking Bengali-English all the time. Only after a few minutes did he notice that all the men were wearing leg-shackles and chains. We had never heard of anyone before jumping over a prison wall to get on the inside!

A good-sized clinic has grown from putting a Band-Aid on the cut finger of a local carpenter.

Now, volunteers hold clinic hours twice each day, and the Peace Corps physician comes twice a week for serious cases.

The mason is becoming a proficient lab technician in his spare time, the mechanic is learning enough first-aid to be an excellent medic, the carpenter is finding out more and more about diseases that he never before knew existed. The sociologist has so far given over fifty injections and is going out of his mind trying to keep medical records—all the more complicated by the fact that many of the patients have identical Moslem names. From one or two patients a day that came in January, a typical day a month later had 67 cases of fungus, systemic infections, worms, cut hands and feet, and countless other maladies. The clinic has been good for the Pakistani people since all other forms of medical care in that area were nonexistent. It has been good for the Peace Corps since it has broken down the barriers between the volunteers and the local population. It has been beneficial for us for these reasons as well as seeing the effectiveness of proper medication in an amazingly short period of time.

The people are curious, friendly, smiling, singing, wanting to share, eager to learn, willing to teach, and extremely tolerant of our ignorance of their culture. And the land is lush and flat and serene. Among such a people and such a land, the PCV's have settled down to work.

JIM BAUSCH

143

What Is an Educational Aide?
by LEONARD GIESEKE,
Volunteer in the Philippines

Upon arriving in the Philippines, we were asked again and again, "What is the Peace Corps going to do here?" We had a ready answer: "We are here as teachers' aides in English and science." But what was a teacher's aide?

We knew what it was not. There is an oversupply of teachers in the Philippines—an oversupply in terms of more teachers than there is money to hire. Because of this, it was made clear we were not to be teachers regularly handling classes. There was no intention that we should take jobs—though only potential jobs—from Filipinos. Only half-jokingly was it suggested that we would do such things as erase blackboards.

In the teaching of English the role was defined. We were to be models of spoken English, to be called upon to recite before the class for imitation by the students. Not an exceptionally challenging role—rather like self-propelling tape recorders—but a role which we could at least understand and explain. We did not feel very challenged, nor were we particularly convinced that it was necessary that Filipinos speak American English. In the area of Los Baños, where we were trained in the Philippines, there is spoken Filipino English. It is at least as intelligible to most Americans as Brooklyn English is to a Georgian.

In science our role was less defined but the contributions we could make were more obvious. Science tends to be neglected in the schools because the teachers lack training in it. The Division of Science of the Bureau of Public Schools is aware of this problem but the solution is slow. There are not enough scientists in the Philippines to provide adequate training.

But as we left for the barrios, we were doubtful that we would be able to contribute very much to the Philippines. We faced, we thought, a limited role.

All of us were wrong.

We found and are finding in the barrios more creative opportunities, more opportunities to contribute than we had imagined. In the schools, the vaguely defined role of teachers' aides is being defined by each volunteer in terms of his abilities and the need of the school in which he is working. In some schools, English teaching is adequate, but in some spoken English is unintelligible, the local dialect too strongly influencing it. English is important for two reasons. First it is the only language spoken throughout the Philippines. There are between 80 and 90 different dialects spoken here and a lack of English severely restricts the geographical area in which a Filipino may comfortably travel or work. Second, the language used in high schools and colleges is English. In science we were already aware of the need, and the limitation we had feared in the teacher's aide concept is being resolved. By working with the students on individual projects and outside of class, by working with the teachers in designing experiments which utilize materials available in the communities, the volunteers have found a creative and useful role in the teaching of science in the schools.

In addition, in the schools and the communities in which we live, we are finding myriad opportunities to be of use. Some are organizing libraries and reading centers. Others are designing and laying out recreational facilities. Some are helping in the campaign to arrest the spread of cholera, while a few are helping in agricultural experimentation. One group has even started adult education classes at night.

To the question, "What are the Peace Corps volunteers going to do here?" we can say "We are here to serve as teachers' aides in the elementary schools and to be participating members of the communities in which we live." The last half of the answer deserves as much emphasis as the first.

PART FOUR

ORGANIZATION AND

ADMINISTRATION

CHAPTER 1

CONTROL AND STRUCTURE

What is the form of the Peace Corps? Before its founding, suggestions ran the gamut from wholly private to wholly governmental.

For a time, a decentralized "Peace Corps Foundation" was under serious consideration. It would have been on the model of the National Science Foundation and, like it, administered by a Presidentially appointed board of private citizens. Father Theodore Hesburgh, president of Notre Dame University, and Thomas Melady, a prominent consultant on Africa, were among its early supporters.

The advantages of this approach are many. Private groups bring to the Government experience and know-how, a self-reliant independence, established procedures and contacts, a notable lack of bureaucratic red tape, and a ready pool of trained technicians. Also, the grass-roots basis of their operations had already won them acceptance in neutral circles not always so friendly to Americans.

However, there are disadvantages as well. The present structure of private programs is inadequate

149

to handle a venture as large as the Peace Corps. The changes necessary in administration and organization might not appeal to them. And, in many cases, groups jealous of their independence would be reluctant to make their goals conform to the needs and purposes of the U. S. Government.

The deciding factors, however, which caused the Administration to veto a private foundation were:

1. It would compete with existing foundations.
2. If sponsored by government and private enterprise alike, it would be resented by agencies wholly dependent on private subscription. The Eisenhower "People-to-People" program failed partly because it alienated private groups in this way.
3. Congress would be reluctant to put money *carte blanche* into programs it does not control.
4. The Constitution specifies that a) the President has full responsibility for the conduct of U. S. foreign policy, and b) a clear line of authority must run from him to those responsible to him. A Peace Corps Foundation would fail on both counts.

The wholly governmental approach, favored by the AFL-CIO and some liberal student groups, was also rejected. It was felt that adding another new bureaucracy would be a sure way to lose the "grassroots" appeal of the Peace Corps. Besides, there would be no advantage in failing to utilize the parent voluntary agencies, and thus antagonize one of the principal sources of support.

The Peace Corps Act established the agency as semi-autonomous within the State Department. The Director reports directly to the Secretary of State. Despite the opposition of former ICA Director Henry Labouisse, the Peace Corps was not merged with the new Agency for International Development (AID), the all-inclusive foreign aid program set up by President Kennedy. This was a victory for Sargent Shriver and other Peace Corpsmen who agree with Asian and African leaders that its special identity and *esprit de corps* would be lost in a massive bureaucracy. Further, the semi-independence of the Peace Corps lessens the possibility that it will be identified with the Cold War aspects of the Mutual Security Program.

The advantages of the Peace Corps Foundation are preserved in two ways. As a compromise, the Advisory Council, headed by Vice-President Lyndon Johnson, includes representatives of educational institutions, private voluntary agencies, farm groups and labor unions. And the effort is diversified among both government and nongovernment channels, of which there are five: the private voluntary agencies; universities and colleges; United Nations agencies; AID and other U. S. agencies; and direct Peace Corps units.

The Private Voluntary Agencies

Because these groups have many continuing projects and are already established in many underdeveloped countries, the Peace Corps has contracts with them for carrying out projects which it will negotiate in their behalf with foreign governments. Another possibility is the initiation of projects by the private agencies themselves. For this, they first submit a prospectus of specific operation, and if the Peace Corps approves, the project will be submitted to the government of the host country for negotiation of details.

Sargent Shriver has called upon other private groups, notably the business and labor communities, to supply Peace Corpsmen. He sees American private enterprise contributing their services in public administration and industrial management as government interns, accountants, administrative assistants, statisticians and clerical personnel. It is commonplace that the governments, both national and local, of underdeveloped countries do not have the organizational know-how for the wide range of services with which they must provide their people. Labor groups can supply such skills as plumbers, electricians, transport workers, and teachers for technical trade schools.

Controversy has arisen from time to time over the similar use of religious organizations, which account for a large percentage of the private voluntary agencies. The Peace Corps has refrained from contracts with directly religious-affiliated groups because of this. Some argue that the advantages would outweigh the possible perils, because they believe that the Peace Corps has cheated itself out of a great resource.

The World Council of Churches, a Protestant and Eastern Orthodox association, has, for the most part, backed the Peace Corps stand from the beginning. It has been wary of contracts with government agencies for two reasons. First, on the score of the constitutional requirement for separation of church and state. Second, for the churches' sake: any possibility that the separate identities and missions of the churches and the Federal Government might be confused has to be scrupulously avoided. On the practical side, this is easy to understand. In Moslem and Hindu countries, for example, a Christian religious group might run the risk of embarrassing the Peace Corps. On the other hand, no churchman would like being considered a part of U.S. foreign policy.

Colleges and Universities

Since 1938, the State Department has operated a limited Peace Corps type of program under the International Educational Exchange. As the name suggests, it has been a two-way venture, making grants to both American and foreign teachers to teach for a year in an elementary or secondary school or to lecture at a university or serve as a consultant abroad. In 1961, 57 universities had contracts with federal agencies for educational projects in 37 countries, and Teachers College at Columbia University supplied more than 150 English teachers for service in East Africa.

One of the principal uses of colleges besides teaching is training, research, and project evaluation for the Peace Corps. Many colleges also have unique resources for recruiting purposes. Some educational institutions and regional associations have departments devoted to Peace Corps information.

In the past, three types of contracts with universities existed. The old Technical Co-operation Administration (TCA) used the device of borrowing the services of university personnel for duty overseas. It was a relatively short-term operation.

The second type employs a university to maintain a technical mission as part of a foreign country's over-all development program. The faculty selected might operate an agricultural extension service, as in the case of land-grant colleges, or as a teacher training team under the country's ministry of education.

The third type is a university-to-university exchange, primarily one in which educational and university administration techniques are supplied.

It might be supposed that university contracts would be the most likely to succeed. However, as Harlan Cleveland noted, the internationalization of colleges has not kept up with the swift pace of world events. At times contract work has been unsatisfactory because the university had accepted it primarily for prestige value, and then relegated it to a low position on its priority list of jobs to be done. In many other cases, it has been the fault of the Federal Government in assigning complex foreign affairs work to colleges ill-equipped to handle it.

The Peace Corps has had a few disappointing experiences along these lines, particularly with certain larger, prestige-conscious universities. In an interview with *The New York Times*,[1] Associate Director Lawrence Dennis emphasized that the Peace Corps could not fulfill its mission without the help of educational institutions, because it "never intended and does not now intend to build up a large training faculty of its own." But, he continued, some universities with heavy backlogs of federal grants "saw the Peace Corps as just another subject for research projects and . . . as just another source of federal grant funds." Best co-operation, he said, came from smaller colleges which, like the Peace Corps, were "volunteer-centered, not faculty-centered or institution-centered." The most common complaint by volunteers was that those university programs which proved unsatisfactory concentrated too much on the theoretical aspects and not enough on the "meat" of the project assignment. In all fairness, however, part of the blame lies with the Peace Corps—and innocently so. In the early months of its existence, the Peace Corps did not have enough experience with which to guide the colleges in setting up just the right training programs. But, on the whole, for a program which is still very much in the experimental stage, university performance has been topnotch. Mr. Dennis selected Texas Western College and the University of Northern Illinois for special commendation in their work with volunteers.

[1] December 30, 1961.

In addition, programs of inter-university area co-operation have been set up. In Washington, D.C., seven—Howard, Georgetown, American, Catholic, George Washington, Maryland, and Johns Hopkins —have pooled their faculties to train volunteers. The first year involved eleven projects, ranging from teachers for Ethiopia to fishermen for Togo. Similarly, the University of Puerto Rico, the Inter-American University, and Catholic University of Puerto Rico jointly administer the training of community development workers bound for Latin America.

One novel feature of the Peace Corps' academic program was the contract with Ohio University for a teacher project in the West African Republic of Cameroun. Optional academic credit was offered to volunteers while overseas. The stipulations of the contract, which promises to be a model for like projects, are:

1. All candidates for further academic credit studies must have a bachelor's degree to qualify. Those who qualify register with the university for the courses of their special interest.

2. Each volunteer opting for the program is charged at the standard Ohio University rate for the first three-hour course in which he may enroll, either in independent study or in a correspondence division course. Upon successful completion of this first course, all further course work which he may undertake during his tour of duty is provided by the university on a tuition-free scholarship basis.

3. Normally no volunteer is permitted to complete more than six semester hours of regular course work per academic year. For the two-year tour of duty, twelve credits is the maximum.

4. An exception to the above stipulation is the special program in student teaching. Students who a) desire credit for student teaching, and b) have successfully completed at least six semester hours of course work in the standard pre-student-teaching sequence before December 1, 1963, may participate for credit in the special student teaching program. An Ohio University representative in Cameroun will direct this program from January to June, 1964.

Several studies have suggested that preparation for Peace Corps work should begin before graduation. Specifically, they recommend special undergraduate courses of intensified language instruction, social science, area studies, particular and comparative civilization, and teacher training. Georgetown University's School of Foreign Service and American University's School of International Service prepare students for the diplomatic corps and for international trade. Present programs in institutions of this sort are being expanded and geared to Peace Corps needs to provide a ready pool of recruits.

U. S. Government Agencies

Although U. S. foreign aid experts have departed from their traditional aloof role as advisers and have been drawn into the actual operation of technical assistance, there is still a wide gap between what they can do and what their native staff does. Often an underdeveloped country is so short of qualified manpower that the AID adviser-technician does not have a staff of any sort. In his initial report to the President, Sargent Shriver underscored the need for "technician-helpers" to supplement the federal agencies' operations at the working level. Holland and West Germany have, for several years, supplied "junior experts" to do similar work abroad. One area where they might serve, as Senator Hubert Humphrey has pointed out, is with the U. S. Information Agency (USIA) as English instructors and junior librarians to staff literacy and information centers in the less accessible parts of a foreign country. This is feasible, he added, so long as the volunteers do not become involved in the propaganda end of USIA, which is admittedly America's official public relations firm —propaganda would be an adventure fatal to the Peace Corps mission.

Directly Administered Peace Corps Units

The cautious pioneer report of Professor Max Millikan, of the Massachusetts Institute of Technology, urged against direct Peace Corps projects. He feared the heavy hand of bureaucracy in government programs, while another skeptical educator commented that the provision is merely a convenient loophole to be used later on as an excuse to transform the entire effort into a wholly governmental operation. The Peace Corps vehemently denies that this is so, and they point to the 17 projects which have, to date, been assigned to private voluntary groups alone. Shriver explains that there are "some projects of a size or complexity or novelty or urgency which cannot be carried out, or carried out well, through any of the usual channels." The first Peace Corps project, road construction in Tanganyika, is apparently of this type. Work is being done there by a team of surveyors, geologists and civil engineers, and an important side effect is the training of young Tanganyikans in surveying techniques so that they can take over when the Peace Corps "phases out."

The United Nations

The possibilities of Peace Corps–United Nations co-operation are explored in Part Five of this book.

Cost and Financing

Under the Peace Corps Act, the Director seeks appropriations yearly from Congress. Because the agency is semi-autonomous, its requests and annual reports are given consideration separate from those of the Agency for International Development.

In June, 1961, the first volunteers were selected. In the four months preceding, the Peace Corps had spent less than $2,000,000—or, as Mr. Shriver assured an economy-minded Republican senator, "something less than the cost of one trial firing of an Atlas missile at Cape Canaveral." These funds were authorized *pro tempore* by the President's

Executive Order setting up the Peace Corps. Total expenses for the period June, 1961, to June, 1962, came to almost $600,000 less than the $30 million appropriated by Congress.

Costs were higher during the first year of service, but the Peace Corps has come up with what it considers a realistic approximation of how much each volunteer's two-year tour of duty costs the taxpayer.

Training	$ 2,500
Transportation	2,600
Living allowance	3,100
Clothing	200
Housing	800
Medical care	600
Project equipment and materials	1,000
Termination pay	1,800
Program support	2,448
Administration	2,952
Total	$18,000

This compares favorably with the fiscal experience of the private voluntary agencies, whose reports, for the most part, did not—as does the Peace Corps'—include overhead costs.

Peace Corps headquarters in Washington employs 275 persons, the limit set by Congress for 1961–62, plus occasional temporary help. These, along with administrative personnel around the globe, account for about 25 per cent of the year's budget.

Costs are being reduced in many ways, and others are under study. Although not required, Tanganyika's government volunteered to provide housing, medical care, transportation within the country, and an extra training course. Support from host governments varies from country to country, and these contributions emphasize the host nation's involvement and responsibility in Peace Corps programs. One suggested method of financing is the use of so-called "counterpart funds," or soft native currency used by certain countries as payment for U. S. loans or grants.

Several American businesses and labor unions have offered to train Peace Corpsmen at their own expense; both groups have conducted intern and apprentice training programs which could be adapted and expanded to meet Peace Corps needs. The Caterpillar Tractor Company has already helped in training diesel mechanics for projects in Tunisia, and the Tennessee Valley Authority is training volunteers for a TVA-like project in the São Francisco Valley of Brazil.

The costs are small in comparison with usual federal expenses, perhaps due to the new agency's habit of "cutting corners" and the absence of high salaries and overseas hardship allowances. Another reason is that the Peace Corps, by its very nature, does not have to compete with private industry for

161

the technicians it requires. The long-run dividends will, in the opinion of both hard-boiled economists and foreign assistance workers, make the Peace Corps' effort more than worth the while.

CHAPTER 2

ADMINISTRATION IN THE HOST COUNTRY

a. Precedents and Guidelines

One of the most important insights the United States has learned from virtually a generation of overseas work is that aid should be seen as technical and economic *co-operation, not assistance*. In every instance, an effort of this nature must be as fully *their* program as *ours*. It is said that no man worth his salt likes charity, and it was never more true than in relations between sovereign nations.

When World War II broke out, the common danger forced the United States and Latin America to recognize their interdependence. President Roosevelt proclaimed his Good Neighbor policy, and Nelson Rockefeller was appointed Co-ordinator of Inter-American Affairs.

Within a short time, Rockefeller saw that each country would require a crash program in three basic areas—health, agriculture, and education. In 1942, he set up the Institute of Inter-American Affairs (IIAA) to carry out the project.

The unique contribution of IIAA was the *servicio,* which is the model for many future Peace Corps operations overseas. The *servicio* operates as a bi-national commission to insure full co-operation between American technicians and their counterparts in the host country. It is set up as an integral, though semi-autonomous, bureau within the appropriate ministry, depending on the type of project. It has four main objectives:

1. The U. S. mission and the host government participate jointly in development operations. Recruiting of local personnel, program and project planning, financing and purchase of necessary supplies, performance and supervision of the individual projects, informing the public and defending the program against criticism—all are tasks which the American and the native staff members should co-operate in doing.

2. In working shoulder-to-shoulder, day by day with his counterpart, the U. S. technician comes to know and understand the man's customs as well as the problems facing his country.

3. Work habits and job techniques can be exchanged to their best advantage and add to the experience of both the U. S. technician and his counterpart.

4. As a direct result, the two are able to combine their know-how and to accomplish much more than if the close association did not ex-

ist. The insight both have gained can ease the task of long-range planning and enable them to take care of emergency situations quickly and efficiently.

The *servicio* may be staffed by U. S. technicians and natives alike, but it should ultimately have only one head. Legally, it must exist as a project agency responsible to the local ministry alone. To make the *servicio* an agency of the American Government would destroy it in the eyes of the people it is supposed to serve.

On the other hand, it is important that the operational freedom of the *servicio* have ironclad guarantees. It must be able to establish its own rules for hiring and firing, its own working procedures and its own fiscal management, independent of those of the parent ministry. The value of this can easily be seen in Latin America, particularly in the not-too-distant past when governments and ministries changed hands on the order of every month or so. If the *servicio* in Peru had not been independent of direct government control, between 1943 and 1954 it would have been at the mercy of twelve different ministers of agriculture! [1]

Who Should Staff the Servicio?

Officers of the *servicio* in past operations have been recruited from the leaders of the U. S. tech-

[1] Philip M. Glick, *The Administration of Technical Assistance: Growth in the Americas* (Chicago: University of Chicago Press, 1957).

nical mission and from members of the host government, the latter constituting the great bulk of the staff. The Colorado State University study has recommended that, in addition, the staff should also include representatives of nongovernmental professions such as businessmen, educators, trade unionists and voluntary agency workers.

Whether or not the director of the *servicio* should be an American or a national of the host country depends on two factors: 1) is a competent national available for the job, and 2) will the *servicio*'s freedom of action continue despite the appointment of a national? For the most part, competent nationals have not been available, and consequently the U. S. mission chief serves as director. Some of the voluntary agencies feel that in the initial operations of the Peace Corps, an American director is a must. Part of this feeling stems from the realization that Congress might hesitate to contribute substantial sums to a *servicio* unless an American controls the way the money is spent. *Since* the *servicio* is jointly financed, with the contribution of the host government usually increasing as the program goes along, it is doubtful that Congress would get its wish regardless of who the director is.

"Phase Out"

At what point does a *servicio* project end and the local ministry take over? This is a very real problem in overseas operations, and many programs make one of two mistakes: either they hold on too long or they let go too soon. The *servicio* itself, being an actual unit in the ministry, is seldom discontinued, but individual projects come and go. Some take longer than others, and so no set timetable exists.

The only reliable rule of thumb is that a project should be transferred to the ministry when it is fully in operation *and* an adequate staff has been given sufficient training to keep the project going and on its toes. It may be necessary to look in from time to time to see that it is actually progressing, but meanwhile the *servicio* should go on to other tasks.

The late Tom Dooley once told of his reaction when he, too, was suddenly faced with the realization that he was no longer needed:

> We explained that our locals had been well trained and that we hoped they would take over from us. I laughingly explained that I had come to give aid to the Lao and had succeeded in working myself out of a job. The Prince exclaimed, "Good!" When he saw my surprise at this he said, "This is what aid should be, Doctor. It should not make the people more dependent upon the aider, or upon the country from which he has come. Aid should work itself into a position where it abolishes any further need of itself." After thinking about this, I agree.[2]

In countries where a severe shortage of high-

[2] Tom Dooley, *The Edge of Tomorrow* (New York: Farrar, Straus, 1958).

level manpower exists or where Peace Corps programs are too small to justify the complex setup of the *servicio*, other instruments should be considered for overseas administration. One device is a "joint fund" to which each government makes contributions. Here the host government exercises control over expenditures, but the U. S. mission has a limited veto as well.

b. The Present Setup

For the manner in which the Peace Corps has so far carried out these guidelines for overseas administration, there is no more concise explanation than the agency's own, as spelled out in the 1962 Congressional presentation:

> The Peace Corps has conducted a nation-wide "talent search" to obtain people who are both highly qualified and committed to Peace Corps ideals for service on its overseas staff.[3]
>
> On matters concerning his job, the volunteer is responsible directly to his host country supervisor. The Peace Corps representative in each country is responsible for the general performance, behavior, and welfare of all the volunteers there. Accordingly, he maintains contact directly or through staff or volunteer leaders—with both the volunteer and his supervisor in order to evaluate the volunteer's performance and deal with difficulties before they become major problems.

[3] See Part Two, Chapter 1: *Who Should Serve?*, "Selection of Leaders."

The Peace Corps representative reports to the Ambassador. He has primary responsibility for all Peace Corps relationships with the host country as well as the entire range of Peace Corps activities. These include program development and operations, field negotiation, and co-ordination of all aspects of the Peace Corps program as it may exist or be developed.

The Peace Corps representative is responsible for providing the imagination and ingenuity necessary to retain the freshness and uniqueness of the Peace Corps and keep its objectives clear and its organization appropriately modest.[4] For the Peace Corps to identify as closely as possible with the volunteers and to assure a separate and independent identity for the Peace Corps as a whole, the representative, to the extent possible, carries out all aspects of his responsibilities physically apart from the Embassy and other United States activities. However, he maintains constant and close contact with the Embassy and the AID[5] mission. The Peace Corps representative utilizes, as appropriate, services and facilities of the Embassy and other United States agencies but without too closely identifying the Peace Corps with those agencies. The Peace Corps overseas staffs

[4] This is no theoretical problem. Some time ago, Peace Corps volunteers ran into demands by their non-native supervisors that they live by their lavish standards. In that African country, the European supervisors lived apart from the local populace and belonged to "white-only" social clubs, a hangover from colonial days. The Peace Corpsmen faced the decision of either disobeying their supervisors and toeing the Peace Corps line or cutting themselves off from Africans.

[5] I.e., the Agency for International Development, the new U. S. foreign aid organization.

are expected to live simply and without ostentation. They do not receive post allowances, supplementary post allowances, transfer allowances, separate maintenance allowances, or the post differentials ordinarily paid to Foreign Service and AID overseas employees. Nor may they utilize commissary or PX facilities except with the express authorization of the Director of the Peace Corps.

The Peace Corps representative is given authority to reassign volunteers within the host country, or to recommend that Peace Corps headquarters in Washington assign them to duties in another country or bring them home. In case of emergency, the representative or the Ambassador may direct a volunteer to return to the United States immediately. The representative also approves requests of volunteers to marry.

Peace Corps representatives are assisted, in many instances, by volunteer leaders.

Section 6 of the Peace Corps Act provides for the enrollment of volunteer leaders in a ratio not exceeding one to each 25 volunteers in the Peace Corps as a whole. It also provides that volunteer leaders may be selected with spouses and minor children, although this authority is to be exercised only under exceptional circumstances. . . . The Peace Corps has experimented with the selection, training, and use of volunteer leaders in various ways in order to determine which methods are likely to be most effective. In most cases, volunteer leaders for a project have been selected from among the volunteers in training for that project.

That is the Peace Corps overseas today; the method of operation may, in time, vary from place to place. However, regardless of the instrument chosen, the Peace Corps must preserve the joint operation within the host country which is necessary for effective co-operation and ultimate success.

CHAPTER 3

SERVICE IN THE PEACE CORPS: WHO, HOW AND WHERE

How Is a Volunteer Chosen?

Dr. Lowell Kelly, Director of Selection and Testing, answered this question in an interview at his office in Peace Corps headquarters in Washington.

"First, the applicant should fill out a Peace Corps questionnaire, which can usually be obtained at a local post office, university, agricultural station, Civil Service office, 4-H Club, or Union house. Failing that, he or she should write to us here in Washington.

"The questionnaire answers will tell us whether or not the applicant has the basic qualifications. He or she must be at least eighteen years old, an American citizen, have some sort of skill or aptitude which can be used, and be motivated enough to be willing to serve at least two years overseas in a hardship post. In addition, the applicant must be in excellent physical and mental health.

"After we receive the questionnaire, the information is put on IBM cards for computer tapes.

"Then, we check with the people whom the applicant has given as references of character and ability. We send out a form to these individuals, asking them for honest ratings of the applicant's job competence, emotional maturity, general character, and relationship with other people.

"I might say that we have been surprised and grateful at the conscientious manner with which the applicants' references have answered our questions, for we rely heavily on their evaluations. People have written to us saying that, because they consider an assignment with the Peace Corps a post of great responsibility, they're giving more than the usual run-of-the-mill recommendation.

"Sometimes an applicant will ruin his own chances from the very beginning, because he is less than completely honest with us on this score. We are sometimes given unsuitable references (an undependable type, or persons who know the applicant by no more than a nodding acquaintance) such as the governor of the state, or a senator. They are of no use to us.

"After the references are tallied, we can start to make an initial evaluation of the application. During this waiting period, we put the applicant's folder on file; later, we put the individual through various tests, ranging from the standard Peace Corps examination to a psychiatric and physical check-up.

"The results are then put before the assessment division, composed of psychologists, social workers and other qualified personnel. Their evaluation is a stage completely separate from the rest of the selection.

"Through this, we can weed out the obvious misfits—that is, persons with an alcoholic history or an emotionally unstable background. (We have had only one slipup so far, but this person's unsuitability was discovered shortly after he reached his overseas post and he was sent back home.)

"We then consider the skills of the remainder who are basically qualified, and we proceed to classify them for the job best suiting their talents.

"The job of classification is done first by computers, and we believe we are the first government agency to use them in this way. This gives our classification officer a rough idea of the applicant's abilities when he later reviews the data on an individual basis.

"We then check with the program officer of each project, and he gives us a detailed run-down of his needs and requirements in a prospective volunteer. There are certain basic needs for each project—if an applicant lacks even one of these, he is out of the running for that particular job. But he still may be ideally suited for another project.

"An applicant who is considered promising by a program officer is sent a project brochure, amounting to an invitation to join. Acceptance is as high as 90 per cent and as low as 40 per cent, depending on such factors as the time of the year, the general attractiveness of the host country, and the project itself.

174

"If he accepts and is in turn accepted by *all* concerned in the Peace Corps, then the applicant is sent into training, lasting an average of four to six months. Selection and testing, it must be emphasized, continue throughout this training phase. Usually, five out of six trainees are finally accepted as Peace Corps volunteers. The battery of tests and the training which each would-be volunteer has to face provide a good test of who will succeed and who won't."

Length of Assignment

For a long time, there was a debate about how long volunteers should serve. Thelma Howe, an experienced Quaker service official, said that the Friends' experiment has shown that a point of "diminishing returns" was reached when volunteers worked overseas for more than two years. The Near East Foundation, however, disagrees, contending that anything less than three years is inadequate—this was the position of the initial Humphrey legislation of 1960, which specified that a whole year be set aside for training. The preliminary report of Colorado State University argued for a similar program, but it also stated that the Peace Corps must be flexible enough to permit the inclusion of various short-term projects.

The term of service set by the Peace Corps Act is two years, *including* the time allotted for training.

A student once asked Sargent Shriver if it wasn't somewhat expensive to train new people all the time and suggested that the Peace Corps allow volunteers so inclined to re-enlist. Mr. Shriver replied that the idea was under consideration; no decision is forthcoming to date. There are indications, however, that it would not be made a general policy, partially because the Peace Corps Act specifies that the effort is to bring a more widespread exposure of more Americans to other peoples—this might not result if volunteers were to make a career of the Peace Corps. However, requests probably will be considered on an individual basis.

Termination Payment and Allowance

Peace Corpsmen will accumulate $75 a month, payable upon completion of their assignments. In addition, they are paid $2 a day while in training, and they are provided a modest subsistence allowance on a level with that of their counterparts in the host country. This allowance ranges from $70 in the Philippines to $168 in Tanganyika. Volunteers also receive 30 days leave a year—at the rate of 2½ days per month of satisfactory service. An additional $5 a day is provided while on leave.

While overseas, volunteers have no diplomatic privileges or immunities, nor do they have PX privileges. Housing, food, medical care and insurance are covered by their allowance. Disabilities suffered while on Peace Corps duty will entitle volunteers to post-service care and compensation.

Volunteer leaders receive slightly higher allowances and readjustment bonuses, plus additional costs incurred for dependents. Their termination payment is $100 for each month of service.

Insurance is provided volunteers and leaders alike by Travelers Insurance Company, with a $10,000 death benefit protection for each. To pay for it, the full premium of $1.20 per month is deducted from the volunteer's accumulated pay.

The Draft and Military Service

When President Kennedy first proposed the Peace Corps, he suggested it might serve as an alternative to military service. The storm of protest aroused both at home and abroad caused him to drop the idea like a hot potato. An African newspaper observed that if the Peace Corps was worth a draft exemption, then it must be tied in with America's mutual security or military defense effort. Lewis Carliner, of the United Auto Workers Union, disputed the "draft-dodging" theory, and replied that many students could not afford two years in the Peace Corps *and* two years in uniform.

The furor quieted down a bit when General Lewis Hershey, Director of the Selective Service, pointed out that service with the Peace Corps—as with comparable overseas work—would entitle volunteers to deferment. Upon their return home, they will probably continue to be deferred because of age and engagement in useful employment.

Applicants who are military reservists must have completed their initial required period of active duty before they can be considered for the Peace Corps. After this is completed, the remainder of obligated weekly drills and two-week active duty tours each year are suspended while serving in the Peace Corps.

What Happens after the Peace Corps Service?

When his enlistment is up, the Peace Corpsman will receive his termination pay, which can be used to tide him over until he finds a job. Later, the Peace Corps hopes to have a career-planning board to seek out prospective employers and to explain to them the nature of the volunteer's experience and performance overseas. In light of the training and experience, no job difficulties are expected; in fact, the Peace Corps expects that ex-volunteers will be in great demand.

Some have suggested that the Peace Corps adopt the program used by Standard Oil of New Jersey. When one of their men is abroad for any great length of time, he is paid at local salary rates, similar to the Peace Corpsman's allowance but not quite so meager. And when he returns home after two to six years' absence, the company credits him with seniority for the time spent overseas, and his full American salary for the entire period is paid to him.

However, the primary hope of the Administration, as stated earlier, is that former Peace Corpsmen will enrich their country by entering U. S. Government or similar international service. Some, perhaps, could rejoin the Peace Corps as training instructors or as Peace Corps representatives overseas. Former Secretary of State Christian Herter has observed that the Peace Corps will benefit the United States as much as, perhaps more than, the nations which are now receiving American aid. It may not be unrealistic, then, to suggest that the Peace Corps youths of today are America's better-prepared leaders for tomorrow.

PART FIVE

THE PROSPECTS: A

WORLDWIDE EFFORT?

In April, 1961, U. S. Ambassador Adlai Stevenson urged the United Nations to co-operate with the American Peace Corps. The proposal was warmly received by the Afro-Asian neutral bloc. After Mr. Stevenson's speech, it was publicly suggested that the United Nations should incorporate the Peace Corps as an international agency.

Is an International Peace Corps, as such, feasible? The Peace Corps in Washington reports that it rejected the proposal in the early days of its existence. Eighty per cent of the private voluntary agencies agree that it is not feasible, although they back the idea in principle.

There is a considerable body of opinion, on the other hand—particularly in international diplomatic circles and among liberal political groups—which sharply disagrees with the official Peace Corps policy. The size of any technical co-operation mission, they argue, depends on five factors: the availability of qualified volunteers, leaders, suitable projects, training staff and facilities, and, last but not least, money. And, with the almost insuperable challenge of bringing nearly two-thirds of the world out of the Stone Age and into the twentieth century, it strains credibility to expect that the United States can do the job alone. So, it is said, an International Peace Corps is a must.

But can the United Nations do it? The UN Expanded Program of Technical Assistance has been declining in scope and importance in comparison with nation-to-nation and regional aid programs. At its best, United Nations Expanded Program of Technical Assistance has never been able to raise in voluntary subscription more than $34 million— with the United States supplying roughly half of this sum. The UN has adequate machinery to set up an International Peace Corps, but it is doubtful that it could come up with the necessary funds.

Some say that an International Peace Corps would strengthen the UN and its specialized agencies. But how true is this? If the United States had to bail it out half the time, wouldn't this actually work to compromise the United Nations? On several different occasions, the United States has volunteered the funds necessary for a particular UN project, but most of the time this has caused even friendly neutrals to question American motives and the propriety of such conduct. The Cold War is a reality, and nothing is accomplished by ignoring it.

On a point of procedure, multilateral agreements of the kind that would have to be negotiated are more painful than pulling a tooth. The 99-plus interests in the UN GENERAL ASSEMBLY must all be pacified, and often the resultant compromise is almost beyond recognition. The American Peace Corps requires only nation-to-nation negotiations, and even its agreements usually undergo considerable revision before they are finally put into effect.

However, no one will deny that the United States can alleviate but a small portion of the immense problems confronting the underdeveloped two-thirds of the globe. If India, for example, wants to raise her daily diet by as little as 100 calories—the equivalent of a single slice of bread—she must have over 5 million more tons of food grains each year. The problem has caused strong men to flinch. Norman Cousins tells of such a man, a young American who quit India after only five months' service. "It's no use," he said. "You help one man only to discover fifty men standing behind him. Then you help fifty men and five thousand suddenly appear. You help the five thousand but what do you do about the five million behind them and the fifty million to follow? At some point along the line you decide it's hopeless." [1]

Someone has to do it, though. The rest of the world—neither prosperous Western Europe nor economically up-and-coming Soviet Russia—cannot just stand by and watch as the gap between the rising expectations and the insufficient resources of the underdeveloped world widens. For human misery, Europe need look no farther than its own

[1] "Confrontation," *Saturday Review*, March 25, 1961.

backyard. In Sicily, home of the Mafia, unemployment and poverty run rampant, and half of the available labor force of Palermo alone is without jobs and adequate food and clothes.[2] Neither are Albania and Bulgaria shining examples of Communist success, any more than Sicily is a showcase of Western private enterprise.

Many of the medium skills that are needed could be provided by the U. S. Peace Corps—but there aren't that many skilled personnel available in the United States.

What then can be done? For one, UN member states could lend junior technicians to projects of the specialized agencies, especially the International Labor Organization, the Food and Agriculture Organization, the World Health Organization, and the UN Economic, Social and Cultural Organization—known respectively as the ILO, FAO, WHO, and UNESCO.

The Peace Corps has adopted this course, and will assign up to 125 volunteers to UN international organizations. The first such project assigned twenty agricultural technicians to serve with the FAO. The job to be done in this case is to help Pakistani farmers along the Ganges and Kobadak rivers to improve their farming methods, at least enough to grow a second crop each year. The Peace Corps–FAO effort follows up the work of several years' heavy investment by the United States and the United Nations in dams and other irrigation

[2] See *Report from Palermo* (Orion: 1959), by Danilo Dolci.

facilities—the volunteers' job, in short, is to translate hydroelectric power and hitherto untapped resources into more food and perhaps cash savings for Asian peasants.

This is one way, and Ambassador Adlai Stevenson has suggested that nations providing volunteers in this manner should assume all maintenance allowances, transportation and other major costs, while, as Tanganyika has done, the countries receiving the aid should help with local expenses. Expenses for the central administration of a UNEPTA effort of this sort should, he added, "as far as possible be a charge of the regularly assessed budgets of the UN."

Two other ways to reduce the unilateral character of foreign technical assistance are being discussed. The first would be to organize international teams either on the basis of regional groups such as the Organization of American States or to coordinate the activities of such private foreign enterprises as the British Voluntary Services Overseas and the German Council for Development Aid.

The second solution is for other nations to set up their own "Peace Corps"—Norway followed the American example by a few months, and several other countries have either indicated an interest or have encouraged privately run organizations to provide similar services.

Whether or not the United Nations establishes an International Peace Corps is, at this point, largely academic. So far, in the judgment of ex-

187

perts and public alike, the new U. S. agency is at least a qualified success.

The rest of the world is watching the Peace Corps. If it is well managed and fulfills the promise of its name, it will be partly because its volunteers and administrators worked cautiously but boldly, with tact every step of the way. But *their* success depends on public support and interest. The Peace Corps is a small contribution toward world understanding and co-operation, but its ultimate impact could conceivably be similar to the Marshall Plan which rejuvenated postwar Europe. If it fails, the immediate impact of its failure might be as little significant as the ripples in a pond, but the final result could be vastly different—the decline of the democratic ideal.